SOFTWARE GUIDE

Using dBASE III PLUS

Ernest S. Colantonio

University of Illinois

D. C. HEATH AND COMPANY

Lexington, Massachusetts Toronto

Photo Credits

Figures 1.2, 1.3, 1.7, and 1.8(d) courtesy of International Business Machines Corp.
Figure 1.4 courtesy of Intel.
Figure 1.5 courtesy of Memorex.
Figure 1.6 courtesy of Seagate Technologies.
Figures 1.10(b) and 1.11 courtesy of Hewlett Packard.

IBM PC is a registered trademark of International Business Machines Corporation.
dBASE III PLUS is a registered trademark of Ashton-Tate Corporation.

Copyright © 1989 by D. C. Heath and Company.

Published simultaneously in Canada.

Printed in the United States of America.

International Standard Book Number: 0-669-19956-7

10 9 8 7 6 5 4 3 2 1

Preface

In this day and age, it's become increasingly evident that a truly general education must include some exposure to computers. Fortunately, microcomputers have become so inexpensive that literally millions of them have surfaced in homes, schools, offices, and businesses everywhere. What's more, they're being used by people from all walks of life. For most of us, being able to use a computer for daily tasks means learning to use prewritten software. Although there are thousands of different programs available for every conceivable purpose, operating systems and data base management packages stand out as two of the most important. Being able to use these types of software is quickly becoming essential for students, professionals, and home users.

The Purpose of This Guide

This guide can be used in any introductory class that teaches the use of these two specific types of software:

1. IBM PC-DOS or MS-DOS
2. dBASE III PLUS

Its lessons teach the student, in a hands-on, step-by-step approach, how to apply these programs to common tasks. For the greatest understanding, students should follow the *Software Guide* as they run the software on their own (or their school's or employer's) computer. On completion of the lessons, the student will be amply prepared to use each of these types of software for common applications.

The Software

The *Software Guide* teaches the use of the world's most popular microcomputer operating system, along with today's best selling data base management program. Although PC-DOS or MS-DOS is not included with this guide, a copy of this operating system is usually purchased as standard equipment with most IBM and IBM-compatible microcomputers. The most recent educational version of the Ashton-Tate package, dBASE III PLUS, is available with this guide.

PC-DOS and MS-DOS 3.30

Almost identical, these twins are the *de facto* standard operating system used on the IBM family of personal computers and compatible machines. Since everyone who uses one of these computers must deal with the operating system to some extent, DOS tops the list of important software to become familiar with. Most of the DOS commands covered in this guide also work with all versions of DOS 2.00 and newer, including IBM DOS 4.00.

dBASE III PLUS

In the minds of many people, dBASE is synonymous with data base management. Sold by Ashton-Tate, dBASE is the most popular programmable, relational data base management system for IBM-compatible computers. It is a very powerful, fast, feature-laden package that is the standard against which all other high-end data base managers are compared. Like other programs with a long history, various versions of dBASE have been released and the system has been consistently improved with each new version. Although dBASE has not always been known for user-friendliness, it is the program of choice for people who need power, speed, flexibility, and programmability in a data base management system. The two most recent versions of dBASE for IBM-compatibles, dBASE III PLUS, and dBASE IV, come with a menu system that makes them much easier to use than earlier, command-oriented versions. In 1987, Ashton-Tate released an Apple Macintosh version, called dBASE Mac, that combines the power of the IBM-compatible dBASE with the ease of use and graphics ability of the Macintosh.

dBASE III PLUS Features

- Full use of the IBM keyboard
- Easy-to-use Assistant menu system
- Quick dot prompt command mode
- On-line help facility
- Data entry forms
- List, browse, retrieve, and display commands to examine existing data base records
- Append command to add new data base records
- Update commands to change existing data base records
- Delete command to remove existing data base records
- Search command to find one or more data base records
- Global update and delete commands to change or remove selected records throughout an entire data base
- Modify command to change the record structure of an existing data base
- Customized report generation
- Data base sorting
- Data base indexing

System Requirements

The following system requirements are needed to use this popular software:

- An IBM or IBM-compatible microcomputer
- MS- or PC-DOS Version 2.00 or higher
- At least 384K RAM
- An 80-column monochrome or color monitor
- A dot-matrix or laser printer
- Two 5¼-inch or 3½-inch floppy disk drives, or at least one floppy disk drive and a hard disk drive (a hard disk drive is recommended)

The Guide

The *Software Guide* is both a user's manual and a workbook with exercises. It is specifically designed to be used with the software described above. This guide, which consists of three parts, covers:

1. An introduction to microcomputers
2. DOS instructions and exercises
3. dBASE III PLUS instructions and exercises

As a user's manual, the *Software Guide* provides an introduction to the specific type of software, a description of its general features, and a series of lessons on how to use these features. As a workbook, the *Software Guide* gives students clear explanations, step-by-step instructions, and plenty of exercises to practice and test their skills. More specifically, it includes:

- Clear learning objectives for each part
- A description of the software's general capabilities
- Carefully paced step-by-step lessons
- Over 150 exercises ranging in difficulty from simple to complex
- Numerous examples
- Answers to multiple choice and fill-in exercises
- Command summaries for DOS and dBASE III PLUS for easy reference
- A comprehensive glossary
- Exceptionally clear, actual screen views

The *Software Guide* can be assigned in class or used in a self-paced lab setting. Either way, the workbook and accompanying software will help students get the software experience they'll need in today's world.

Acknowledgments

Several people were involved in making this project possible. I am especially grateful to Lee Ripley and Pam Kirshen for the original inception of the idea for this guide's predecessors. Their help and support, along with that of Jill Hobbs, was greatly appreciated. Special thanks go to C. Brian Honess of the University of South Carolina for many of the short and long problems which were adapted from the original *Software Guide*. I'd like to thank Peter Gordon of D. C. Heath for his new vision of what these manuals could become, and Kitty Sheehan for handling all of those little details, as well as Cia Boynton, Kathleen Savage, and Irene Cinelli for all the time and effort they contributed toward the completion of this project.

E. S. C.

License Agreement for dBASE III PLUS

Important: Please read this page before using the dBASE III PLUS program, a copy of which is being made available to you for use in conjunction with the Textbook pursuant to the terms of this Agreement for educational, training and/or demonstration purposes. By using the dBASE III PLUS program, you show your agreement to the terms of this license.

Exclusions of Warranties and Limitations of Liability

The copy of the dBASE III PLUS program made available for use with this textbook is a limited functionality version of dBASE III PLUS, and is intended solely for educational, training and demonstration purposes. Accordingly, this copy of dBASE III PLUS is provided "as is," without warranty of any kind from Ashton-Tate or D.C. Heath. Ashton-Tate and D.C. Heath hereby disclaim all warranties of any kind with respect to this limited functionality copy of dBASE III PLUS, including without limitation the implied warranties of merchantability and fitness for a particular purpose. Neither Ashton-Tate nor D.C. Heath shall be liable under any circumstances for consequential, incidental, special or exemplary damages arising out of the use of this limited functionality copy of dBASE III PLUS, even if Ashton-Tate or D.C. Heath has been apprised of the likelihood of such damages occurring. In no event will Ashton-Tate's or D.C. Heath's liability (whether based on an action or claim in contract, tort or otherwise) arising out of the use of this limited functionality copy of dBASE III PLUS exceed the amount paid for this textbook.

Limited Use Software License Agreement

Definitions

The term "Software" as used in this agreement means the Limited Use version of dBASE III PLUS which is made available for use in conjunction with this Textbook solely for educational, training and/or demonstration purposes. The term "Software Copies" means the actual copies of all or any portion of the Software, including back-ups, updates, merged or partial copies permitted hereunder.

Permitted Uses

You may:

- Load into RAM and use the Software on a single terminal or a single workstation of a computer (or its replacement).
- Install the Software onto a permanent storage device (a hard disk drive).
- Make and maintain up to three back up copies provided they are used only for back-up purposes, and you keep possession of the back-ups. In addition, all the information appearing on the original disk labels (including copyright notice) must be copied onto the back-up labels.

This license gives you certain limited rights to use the Software and Software Copies for educational, training and/or demonstration purposes. You do not become the owner of and Ashton-Tate retains title to, all the Software and Software Copies. In addition, you agree to use reasonable efforts to protect the Software from unauthorized use, reproduction, distribution or publication.

All rights not specifically granted in this license are reserved by Ashton-Tate.

Uses Not Permitted

You may not:

- Make copies of the Software, except as permitted above.
- Rent, lease, sublicense, time-share, lend or transfer the Software, Software Copies or your rights under this license except that transfers may be made with Ashton-Tate's prior written authorization.
- Alter, decompile, disassemble, or reverse-engineer the Software.
- Remove or obscure the Ashton-Tate copyright and trademark notices.
- Use the Software or Software Copies outside the United States or Canada.

Duration

This agreement is effective from the day you first use the Software. Your license continues for fifty years or until you return to Ashton-Tate the original disks and any back-up copies, whichever comes first.

If you breach this agreement, Ashton-Tate can terminate this license upon notifying you in writing. You will be required to return all Software Copies. Ashton-Tate can also enforce our other legal rights.

General

This agreement represents the entire understanding and agreement regarding the Software and Software Copies and supersedes any prior purchase order, communication, advertising or representation.

This license may only be modified in a written amendment signed by an authorized Ashton-Tate officer. If any provision of this agreement shall be unlawful, void, or for any reason unenforceable, it shall be deemed severable from, and shall in no way affect the validity or enforceability of the remaining provisions of this agreement. This agreement will be governed by California law.

Contents

Chapter 3   dBASE III PLUS   61

1

The Microcomputer

Learning Objectives

After reading this chapter, you should know the following:

- What is meant by the term *microcomputer*
- The basic operations performed by all computers
- The four major hardware components of a typical microcomputer system
- The major components inside a microcomputer's system unit
- The three major types of microcomputer displays
- How the various special-purpose keys on a microcomputer keyboard are used
- The four most popular types of microcomputer printers
- The three major categories of microcomputer software
- How to turn on a microcomputer
- How to operate a microcomputer printer
- How to care for floppy disks

Introduction

We begin this first chapter by introducing IBM and IBM-compatible microcomputers, their hardware components, and popular types of software. (By *IBM-compatible* we mean any computer that works like a comparable IBM model and can run the same software.) Then we discuss a few helpful hints for working with microcomputers.

What Is a Microcomputer?

Its very name tells us that a **microcomputer** is a small computer, and a **computer** is an electronic device that performs calculations and processes data. Most people think of a microcomputer as being small enough to fit on top of a desk. Although some powerful models can serve several users simultaneously, most microcomputers are used by only one person at a time. For this reason, microcomputers are also often called **personal computers**.

Another characteristic of microcomputers is that their "brain" or **central processing unit (CPU)** consists of a single electronic device known as a **microprocessor**. This device, a marvel of miniature engineering, controls the microcomputer, performs its calculations, and processes data. A microprocessor is just one type of integrated circuit chip, which is a thin slice of semiconductor material, such as pure silicon crystal, impregnated with carefully selected impurities. These chips are commonly used in computers and many other modern electronic devices.

One way to define microcomputers is by what they do. They can be used to help accomplish many different tasks. At the lowest level, however, a microcomputer performs the same basic operations as all computers. This can be summed up as *input*, *processing*, and *output* (see Figure 1.1).

Figure 1.1   What a Computer Does

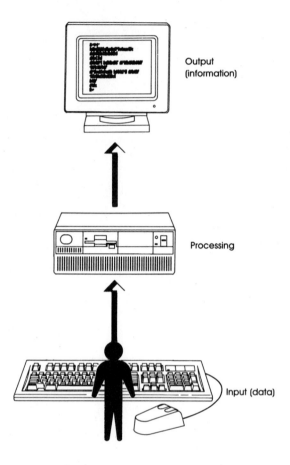

Output (information)

Processing

Input (data)

First, **a program** is needed to tell the computer what to do. This is a set of instructions that controls a computer's operation. The program lets you enter raw **data**, which can consist of numbers, text, pictures, and even sounds. These data entered into the computer are called **input**. The program instructs the computer to process the data by doing calculations, comparisons, and other manipulations. The final result is processed data or **information**, hopefully a more organized and useful form of the original input. This information produced by the computer is called **output**. Keep in mind that there is no magic here—a program is needed to tell the computer what to do and the output information is only as valid as the original input data.

Although microcomputers perform the same basic operations as larger computers, they differ in speed and capacity. Larger computers can generally process data faster than microcomputers. They can also internally store more data at a time than microcomputers. These factors make larger computers better for performing lots of extremely complex and time-consuming computations. Microcomputers are also less adept than larger computers at handling several different users or tasks at the same time. On the other hand, microcomputers are superbly adapted to help with many work-a-day tasks like typing papers, figuring taxes, maintaining mailing lists, sending messages, drawing charts, managing finances, and even playing games.

Finally, microcomputers generally fall within a given price range. This range varies from little as $100 to as much as $15,000. Today the average price of a typical microcomputer used in business is around $2500. This is, however, a good deal less than the cost of much more powerful computers, which may run into many thousands or millions of dollars. Although microcomputers are by no means cheap, their prices have been generally dropping even as their capabilities have increased. For example, in late 1983 the list price of a basic IBM Personal Computer XT was $5675. The list price of its successor, a similarly-equipped IBM Personal System/2 Model 30, was only $2545 when first released in mid 1987. Even though the newer Model 30 costs less than half as much as the old XT, it still has more than twice the speed and storage capacity, along with many other improvements.

Hardware

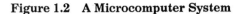

The **hardware** of a computer system is the electronic and mechanical equipment that make it work. Like a stereo system, microcomputer hardware generally consists of several distinct components connected by cables. Although there are several possible arrangements and many different models, Figure 1.2 shows a typical microcomputer system, the IBM Personal System/2 Model 50, which has four major parts: a system unit, display, keyboard, and printer. You will also notice, in this figure, a power switch, a floppy disk drive, and a mouse, all of which will be discussed later.

Figure 1.2 A Microcomputer System

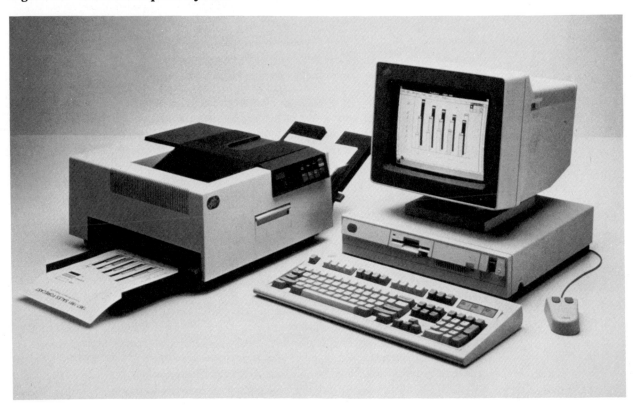

System Unit

From the outside, the system unit looks like a shallow box about the size of a portable typewriter. Figure 1.3 shows what the system unit of an IBM Personal System/2 Model 50 looks like on the inside. This central component houses important elements such as the computer's motherboard, microprocessor, memory, disk drives, and power supply.

Figure 1.3   Inside the System Unit

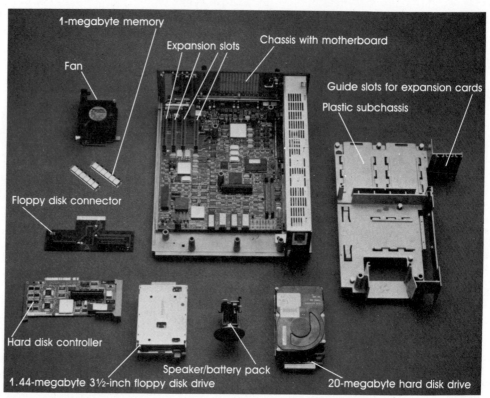

- 1-megabyte memory
- Expansion slots
- Chassis with motherboard
- Fan
- Guide slots for expansion cards
- Plastic subchassis
- Floppy disk connector
- Hard disk controller
- 1.44-megabyte 3½-inch floppy disk drive
- Speaker/battery pack
- 20-megabyte hard disk drive

Motherboard

The main circuit board of a computer is called the **motherboard** or **system board** (see Figure 1.4). Among other components, the motherboard holds the computer's CPU, some memory, and much of its control circuitry. In addition, the motherboard contains the **bus**, a set of wires and connectors that link the CPU to memory and other computer components.

In most microcomputers, the bus is accessible through a series of **expansion slots**. Each expansion slot is an internal connector that allows you to plug an additional circuit board into the motherboard. The IBM Personal System/2 Model 50, for example, has four expansion slots, which can be seen in Figure 1.4. Some computers come with eight or more expansion slots. A circuit board that plugs into an expansion slot is called an **expansion board, card,** or **adapter.** Such circuit boards make it possible to connect a wide variety of extra equipment to a computer, thus *expanding* its capability.

The motherboard or expansion boards also contain device controllers. A **device controller** is a set of chips or a circuit board that operates a piece of computer equipment such as a disk drive, display, keyboard, mouse, or printer. Recently, there has been a trend toward building device controllers onto microcomputer motherboards. The IBM Personal System/2 Model 50 shown in Figure 1.4, for example, has most of its device controllers on the motherboard.

Figure 1.4
A Motherboard
or System Board

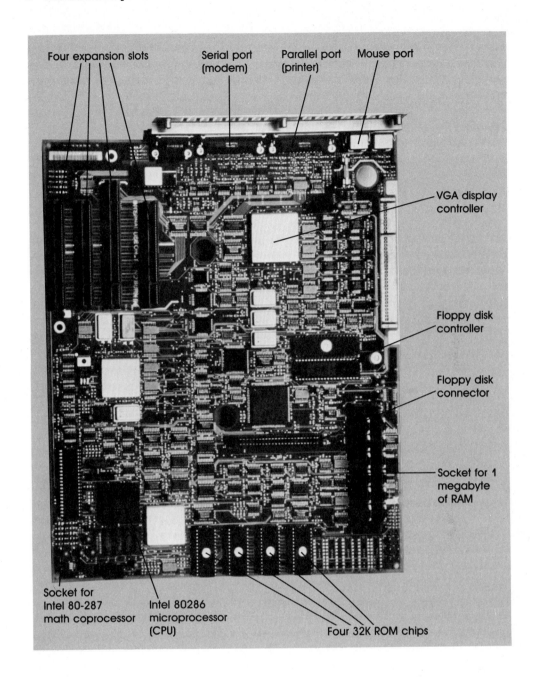

Four expansion slots   Serial port (modem)   Parallel port (printer)   Mouse port

VGA display controller

Floppy disk controller

Floppy disk connector

Socket for 1 megabyte of RAM

Socket for Intel 80-287 math coprocessor   Intel 80286 microprocessor (CPU)   Four 32K ROM chips

Microprocessor

As we said, the microprocessor is a microcomputer's central processing unit (CPU). It consists of a single integrated circuit chip that is usually soldered or plugged into a socket on the motherboard (see Figure 1.4). IBM and IBM-compatible microcomputers use microprocessors from the Intel 8088 family, which includes the 8088, 8086, 80286, and 80386 chips. The 8088 is used in older IBM and IBM-compatibles such as the original IBM Personal Computer and PC/XT. The slightly more efficient 8086 chip is used in IBM's newer low-end models, such as the IBM Personal System/2 Models 25 and 30. The more powerful 80286 chip is used in mid-range microcomputers, such as the original IBM Personal Computer AT and the newer IBM Personal System/2 Models 50 and 60. Finally, the very powerful and fast 80386 chip is used in high-end models, such as the IBM Personal System/2 Models 70 and 80.

Memory

Memory is a computer's internal storage, used to hold programs and data. Also called **primary storage**, memory is measured in bytes. A **byte** is the amount of storage needed to hold a single character, such as the letter A. Since computers can store many thousands or millions of bytes, the terms **kilobyte (K)** and **megabyte (M)** are often used. One kilobyte or 1K is equal to 1024 bytes. One megabyte or 1M is equal to 1,048,576 bytes. In general, microcomputer memory is made up of two types of integrated circuit chips: RAM and ROM.

RAM, which stands for **Random Access Memory**, is temporary storage. Programs and data can be stored there while they are being used and then over-written by other programs and data later. When the computer is turned off, RAM loses its contents. Most microcomputers can now have at least 640K of RAM on their motherboards. Many can have much more installed on expansion boards. For example, the IBM Personal System/2 Model 80 can be equipped with up to 16 megabytes of RAM.

ROM, which stands for **Read Only Memory**, is permanent storage. The contents of ROM chips, which are encoded at the factory, remain intact when the computer is turned off. The programs and data permanently stored in ROM can be read and used, but never erased, changed, or augmented. Many microcomputers use ROM to store programs and data that are used frequently but need never be changed, such as portions of the operating system. Most microcomputers contain at least one ROM chip as part of their primary storage. The IBM Personal System/2 Model 50, for example, uses four 32K ROM chips on the motherboard to store essential programs and data (see Figure 1.4).

Disk Drives

A **disk drive** is a piece of equipment that can read and write programs and data on magnetic disks. A **magnetic disk** is a semi-permanent storage medium that can be erased and rewritten many times. Most microcomputers can now be equipped with two basic kinds of disk drives: floppy disk drives and hard disk drives.

A **floppy disk drive** works with **floppy disks** (also called **diskettes**), which are inexpensive, flexible magnetic disks encased in plastic (see Figure 1.5). Floppy disks can be inserted and removed from their disk drives. The IBM Personal System/2 Model 50, for example, accepts a 3½-inch diskette, which can hold up to 1.44 megabytes of programs and data. Although most newer microcomputers now come with 3½-inch disk drives, many microcomputers still use 5¼-inch floppy disk

Figure 1.5   Floppy Disks

drives. A typical 5¼-inch floppy disk holds 360K, but there are some drives that use 5¼-inch disks that hold 1.2 megabytes.

A **hard disk drive** uses one or more magnetic metal platters to hold programs and data (see Figure 1.6). Most hard disk drives have their magnetic disks permanently sealed inside. These disks are rigid, much faster, and have much greater capacity than floppy disks. Hard disk drives come in sizes ranging from 10 megabytes to several hundred megabytes. The most popular sizes are now 20, 30, and 40 megabytes. The IBM Personal System/2 Model 50, for example, comes standard with a 20 megabyte internal hard disk. On a microcomputer with a hard disk, programs are usually run from the hard disk. The floppy disk drive is generally relegated to copying software to or from the hard disk and making backup copies of important programs and data.

Figure 1.6 Hard Disk Drive

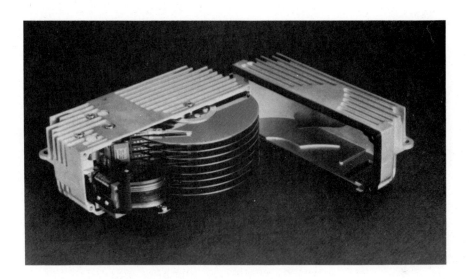

Display

A display, also called a **monitor**, is similar in many ways to an ordinary television screen. The display is used to present text and **graphics**, which are simply any kind of pictures, drawings, charts, or plots. The vast majority of computer monitors create text and graphics on the screen with tiny dots called **pixels** (short for picture elements). The number and size of these pixels determine a monitor's sharpness or **resolution**. There are three basic types of displays:

- **Monochrome Text** These monitors can only display letters, numbers, punctuation, and a limited set of other symbols in just one color, usually green on black, amber on black, white on black, or black on white.
- **Monochrome Graphics** In addition to text, these monitors can also display graphics on the screen. Only one color can be presented, but different shades of that color may be used.
- **Color Graphics** These monitors can display text and graphics in more than one color.

The capabilities of a particular display system are dependent on both the monitor itself and its device controller. The device controller for the display system is called a **display adapter**. For IBM and IBM-compatible microcomputers, there are several different display adapters that can be used. Some of these follow.

- **Monochrome Display Adapter (MDA)** This is the controller used with early low-end IBM microcomputers. It can only display text on a monochrome screen, but it generates very crisp, easy to read characters.
- **Color Graphics Adapter (CGA)** This is IBM's first microcomputer color graphics adapter. It can do color graphics, but the quality is rather poor. In other words, its low resolution makes text and graphics look rather fuzzy. Furthermore, the CGA is limited to a maximum of only 16 different colors, of which only only four can be on the screen at the same time.
- **Hercules Graphics Adapter** This adapter, made by Hercules Computer Technology, acts as a monochrome display adapter, but adds monochrome graphics capability.
- **Enhanced Graphics Adapter (EGA)** This color graphics adapter from IBM can do everything the CGA can do, yet is much better than the CGA. The resolution is significantly higher and the maximum number of different colors on the screen is 16 out of 64 possible choices.
- **Multi-Color Graphics Array (MCGA)** This is the display adapter built onto the motherboards of the IBM Personal System/2 Models 25 and 30. It can be used with either a monochrome graphics or color graphics monitor. It's maximum resolution is better than the EGA and can display a maximum of 256 different colors on the screen at once out of 262,144 possible choices.
- **Video Graphics Array (VGA)** This is the display adapter built onto the motherboards of the IBM Personal System/2 Models 50, 60, 70, and 80. It can also be purchased as a separate expansion board for other types of IBM and IBM-compatible computers. Slightly more advanced than the MCGA, the VGA can also do everything the EGA can do.

Keyboard

The keyboard is the primary device for entering text and telling the computer what to do. It is similar, in many respects, to a typewriter keyboard. Many microcomputers also have an auxiliary input device known as a **mouse**. This little box, which is glided across the table top, allows the user to manipulate objects on the display screen and select actions to be performed by pressing one or more buttons.

For IBM and IBM-compatible microcomputers, there are three basic keyboard designs. These are the original IBM Personal Computer keyboard, the original IBM Personal Computer AT keyboard, and the new IBM Enhanced Keyboard. Figure 1.7 shows all three of these keyboards. Besides the usual letters and punctuation marks that you're likely to find on any typewriter, a computer keyboard has other important keys:

- **Enter (or Return)** Analogous to the carriage return on a typewriter, this key is used to signal the end of an entry. Basically, it tells the computer to go ahead and process what was just typed.
- **Backspace** Like the Backspace key on a typewriter, this key is used to go back and type over a previously typed character.
- **Shift** Located at either side of the keyboard, one of the Shift keys is held down while pressing another key to produce a capital letter or the symbol shown on the top part of the key.
- **Caps Lock** This key is like the Caps Lock key on a typewriter, except that it works for only letter keys. When the caps lock key is pressed, capital letters will appear when you press letter keys. When Caps Lock is pressed again, small letters will appear when their keys are pressed.
- **Tab** Like the Tab key on a typewriter, this key is used to advance to the next tab stop.

**Figure 1.7   (top) Original IBM
PC Keyboard, (center) "AT-
Style" Keyboard, and (bottom)
IBM Enhanced Keyboard**

- **Escape**   The Escape key (abbreviated **Esc**) is often used to cancel a previously typed entry or to prematurely end a program.
- **Break**   This key is very much like the Escape key and is used by some programs in a similar fashion.
- **Control**   Somewhat like a Shift key, the Control key (abbreviated **Ctrl**) is pressed in conjunction with other keys. It's used to control a program's actions by sending certain codes to the computer.
- **Alternate**   Very similar to the Control key, the Alternate key (abbreviated **Alt**) is also pressed in conjunction with other keys. It's used to give an alternate meaning to the keys pressed along with it.
- **Insert**   This key (abbreviated **Ins**) is often used to insert a new entry between existing entries.

■ **Delete** This key (abbreviated **Del**) is often used to erase an entry or a single character.

■ **Function Keys** These are keys that are pressed to activate frequently used operations within a program. They are used differently by different programs. IBM-compatible keyboards have either 10 function keys along the left side or 12 function keys across the top. The function keys are labeled with an F followed by a number, like this: F1, F2, F3, etc.

■ **Cursor Movement Keys** Most programs use these keys to let you move the **cursor** (a little blinking underscore or box) around the screen. In a word processing program, for example, the cursor marks the place where text is inserted, deleted, or otherwise manipulated. The cursor movement keys include Up Arrow, Down Arrow, Left Arrow, Right Arrow, Home, End, Page Up, and Page Down.

■ **Numeric Keypad** This is an array of keys at the right side of a keyboard that resembles the layout of a calculator's keys. It includes the ten digits and other symbols that facilitate the entry of numbers and formulas. On the IBM PC and AT keyboards, the numeric keypad is superimposed on the cursor movement keys.

■ **Num Lock** This key is used to switch the function of the numeric keypad. In one state, the numeric keypad acts as number keys. In the other state, the numeric keypad acts as cursor movement keys. You press the Num Lock key to switch between these two states.

■ **Print Screen** If you have a printer, this key is pressed to send a copy of the current screen to your printer. On some keyboards, it is abbreviated **PrtSc**.

■ **Pause** This key is used to temporarily suspend the operation of the current program.

■ **Scroll Lock** This key is not used by very many programs and it has no standard function. Some programs use it to switch the Cursor Movement keys into a state in which they can move (or scroll) the whole screen up, down, left, or right.

Printer

A **printer** is a device used to produce permanent copies of text and possibly graphics on paper. Although a printer is not absolutely necessary to run most programs, it is an extremely useful addition to a microcomputer system.   This is because computers are commonly used to produce letters, reports, books, tables, figures, charts, graphs, diagrams, maps, and pictures. Paper output, or *hard copy* as it's also called, is a convenient medium for distributing and communicating this work to others. The four kinds of printers most frequently used with microcomputers are dot-matrix printers, daisy-wheel printers, ink-jet printers, and laser printers.

Dot-Matrix Printers

A **dot-matrix printer** is an output device that uses tiny dots to create text and graphics on paper (see Figure 1.8). Just as graphics monitors use pixels to construct characters and pictures on a screen, dot-matrix printers similarly use dots of ink on pages of paper. Inside the dot-matrix printer a *printhead* is moved across the paper from left to right, and sometimes also from right to left (see Figure 1.8). This printhead may contain anywhere from 7 to 27 pins arranged in a vertical column. While most dot-matrix printers use 9 pins, more expensive printers with 18 or 24 pins are also fairly common. As the printhead moves horizontally, it

Figure 1.8 (a) The Printhead of a Dot-Matrix Printer, (b) The Process of Printing a Dot-Matrix Character, (c) The pattern of dots within the matrix that form the character, and (d) An IBM Proprinter XL24, a dot-matrix printer

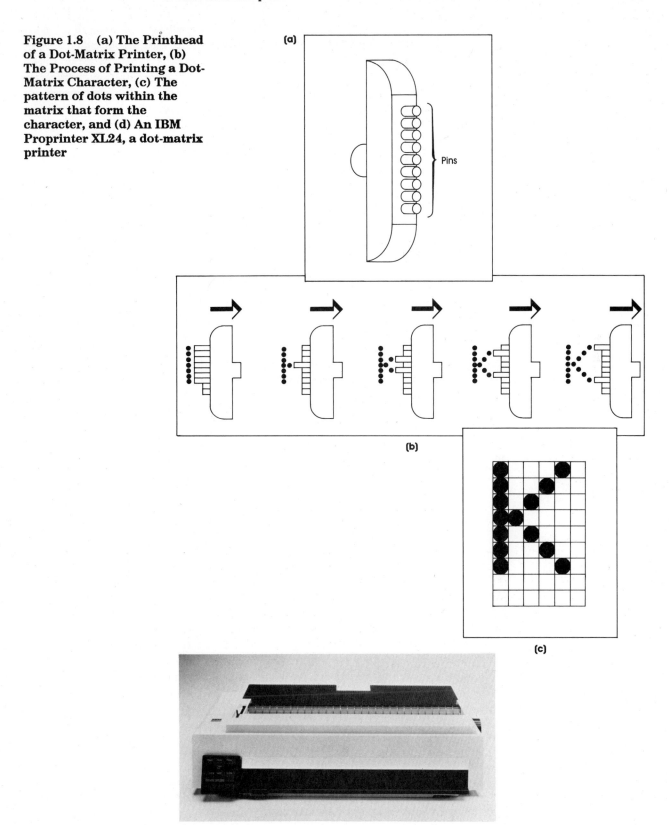

constructs a character by repeatedly striking these pins against an inked ribbon and the paper. Electrical signals cause the appropriate pins to be thrust out at the proper moment to form the successive columns of dots that make up a character's image. Each column of the character is struck in turn against the ribbon and paper until the complete image has been formed. Dot-matrix printers are sometimes described as being impact printers because of the way the pins hit the ribbon and paper. This printing mechanism is most frequently used for text, but dot-matrix printers can usually produce graphics, too.

Dot-matrix printers are by far the most popular type of microcomputer printer. They are reasonably priced, fairly quick, and pretty reliable. Prices range between $150 and $3000, but the typical cost of an average 9-pin dot-matrix printer is about $500. The speed of a dot-matrix printer depends upon what print mode it is using. The fastest mode is called **draft mode**, in which characters are formed by just a single pass of the print head. Some expensive dot-matrix printers are able to achieve speeds of 400 characters per second in draft mode. Many dot-matrix printers also have a **near letter-quality (NLQ) mode**. In this mode, the printhead makes two or more passes over each character, slightly shifting its position each time. This tends to fill in the gaps between the dots and makes text appear more like it was produced by an electric typewriter. Using NLQ mode may slow some printers down to only 15 characters per second. Generating graphics with a dot-matrix printer can also be time consuming. Depending upon how dark the images are, it may take several minutes per page to produce graphics on a dot-matrix printer.

Daisy-Wheel Printers

A **daisy-wheel printer** uses a circular printing mechanism called a **daisy wheel**. Solid, raised characters are embossed on the ends of little "arms" arranged in a circle like the spokes of a wheel or the petals of a daisy. As this daisy wheel spins, a tiny, stationary hammer strikes the back of the proper character when it passes (see Figure 1.9). This impact drives the character pattern, which is embossed in reverse, against an inked ribbon and the paper. Daisy-wheel printers are true **letter-quality** printers because they produce well-defined text just like electric typewriters. Their prices are comparable with that of dot-matrix printers. Unlike dot-matrix printers, however, daisy-wheel printers cannot produce graphics. They are also noisier and slower than dot-matrix printers. The typical daisy-wheel printer can only print about 10 characters per second, and even the most expensive models generally cannot do better than 100 characters per second. Daisy-wheel printers are still fairly popular with microcomputer owners, but they are gradually being supplanted by 24-pin dot-matrix printers and laser printers.

Ink-Jet Printers

An **ink-jet printer** has a mechanism that squirts tiny, electrically-charged droplets of ink out of a nozzle and onto the paper (see Figure 1.10). (No pins or hammers strike the paper, so ink-jet printers are classified as nonimpact printers.) Ink-jet printers are fast, quiet, and can produce high-quality print, but they are slightly more expensive than dot-matrix printers. Some ink-jet printers have a tendency to clog their nozzle with ink and smear characters on paper. Many ink-jet printers, however, have the capability to print in color, a capability most other types of printers lack.

Figure 1.9   The Daisy-Wheel Printing Mechanism and a Daisy Wheel

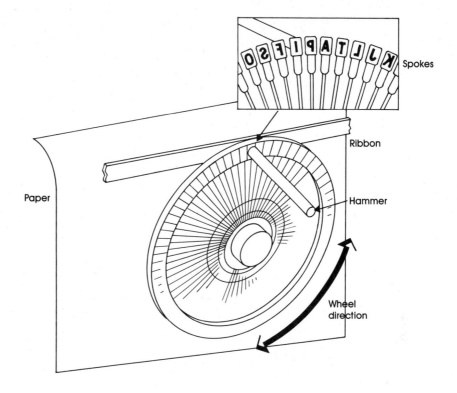

Figure 1.10   (above) Ink Jet Printing, and (below) The Hewlett-Packard PaintJet Color-Graphics Printer

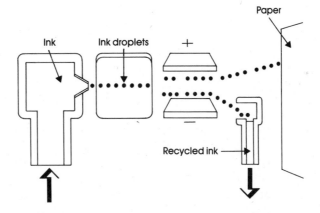

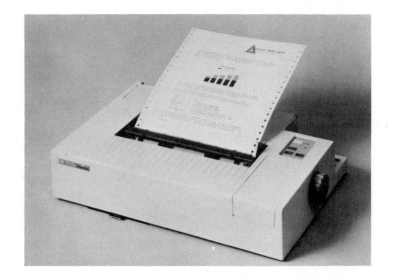

Laser Printers

A **laser printer** is an output device that uses tightly focused beams of light to transfer images to paper (see Figure 1.11). A tiny laser emits pulsating pinpoint bursts of light that are reflected off a special spinning mirror. This mirror reflects light onto a rotating drum. Light striking the drum causes it to become charged with electricity. An inklike toner is attracted to the drum in these electrically charged spots. When the drum is rolled over a piece of paper, the toner is transferred to the paper and an image is permanently fixed through a combination of heat and pressure. This image transfer process is similar to that found in a plain-paper photocopy machine. The result is high-quality text and graphics that almost look as if they were typeset. (Like ink-jet printers, laser printers are classified as nonimpact printers.)

Laser printers represent the most advanced printing technology. Although the images they produce are made up of dots, these dots are much smaller and more densely packed than the dots created with a dot-matrix printer. The typical microcomputer laser printer is capable of printing at a resolution of 300 dots per inch, both horizontally and vertically. This means 90,000 dots per square inch. Besides printing high-quality images, laser printers are also fast and quiet. The average speed of most laser printers is 8 pages per minute. This is equivalent to about 400 characters per second. Because laser printers don't use impact methods like dot-matrix and daisy-wheel printers, they are very quiet by comparison. The major disadvantage to laser printers is their cost. Prices generally start at around $1000. Despite the cost, more and more laser printers are being used with microcomputers every year. They are especially popular in office situations where the printer can be shared among several users.

Figure 1.11   The Hewlett-Packard LaserJet Series II Laser Printer

Software

By itself, computer hardware is useless. Programs are needed to operate the hardware. As we mentioned earlier, a program is simply a sequence of instructions that tells a computer what to do. **Software** is a general term that refers to any single program or group of programs. In contrast to hardware, which is constructed from physical materials like metal and plastic, software is built from knowledge, planning, and testing. A person who creates programs is called a **programmer**. Programmers use their knowledge of how a computer works to plan sets of instructions that accomplish useful tasks. These instructions are entered into the computer and repeatedly tested and modified until they achieve the desired results. As we said earlier, programs and data are generally kept on magnetic disks, where they can be accessed and used over and over again. Note that the disks themselves aren't the software, they're just the medium on which software is stored.

As an analogy, think of a stereo system. The amplifier, compact disc player, and speakers are the hardware. The amplifier is like the central processing unit and memory, the compact disc player is like a disk drive, and the speakers are like the display, except they present audio instead of video output. The music, which is stored on compact discs, is like software, which is stored on floppy disks. Just as you can amass a huge music collection by buying more compact discs, you can build a bigger software library by purchasing additional programs on floppy disks. The stereo system is of little use without the compact discs and the compact discs are useless without the stereo system. Similarly, a computer system is useless without software and software is useless without a computer system on which to run it.

Just as there are different types of hardware, there are also different types of software. Basically, there are three major categories: *system software*, *programming languages*, and *application software*.

System Software

System software handles the many details of managing a computer system. A computer's **operating system** makes up most of its system software. This is the set of programs that controls a computer's hardware and manages the use of software. One small part of the operating system, for example, is a program that identifies which key you've pressed, determines the character that corresponds to that key, and forms that character on the display screen. Another example is a program that lets you erase the contents of a magnetic disk. Some system software is built into a computer's ROM chips, while other system software comes on magnetic disk and must be purchased separately.

Programming Languages

Computer programs are developed with programming languages. A **programming language** is simply a set of symbols and rules to direct the operations of a computer. There are many different programming languages in common use, each designed to develop certain types of programs. A few of the most popular programming languages are BASIC, Pascal, C, FORTRAN, COBOL, and Ada. Although it can be helpful to learn a programming language for some very specific applications, most people who use computers don't actually program them. They just use programs, such as operating systems and application software, that have been developed by professional programmers.

Application Software

Application software is the software that applies the computer to useful tasks such as helping you create documents, figure your taxes, maintain mailing lists, and draw charts. Also called **application packages** or simply **applications**, these programs are the real reason most people buy and use microcomputers. The three most widely used applications follow.

- **Word Processing** A **word processing package** is software that helps you prepare documents by letting you enter, store, modify, format, copy, and print text.
- **Spreadsheet** A **spreadsheet package** is software that lets you manipulate tables of numbers, text, and formulas. It is an extremely flexible tool that can be used to handle typical accounting chores, monitor investments, balance a checkbook, and work out a budget.
- **Data Base Management** A **data base** is an organized collection of one or more files of related data. A file is a mass of individual data items kept together on a disk. A **data base management package** is software that lets you create, add to, delete from, update, rearrange, select from, print out, and otherwise administer data files such as mailing lists and inventories.

Besides these "big three" application packages, there are many other types of popular software, including the following:

- **Communications** Using an auxiliary device called a **modem**, a computer can transmit and receive programs and data over ordinary telephone lines. Communications software makes it possible for a computer to use a modem to call other computers and access on-line information services.
- **Graphics** Graphics packages let you use a computer to create all kinds of pictures including graphs, charts, maps, paintings, drawings, diagrams, blueprints, simulated slide shows, and animated presentations.
- **Desktop Publishing** Combining the results of word processing and graphics, desktop publishing or page layout software lets you use a computer and laser printer to produce near typeset quality documents.
- **Accounting** Accounting software lets you use a computer to record, analyze, and report business transactions.
- **Integrated Software** Integrated software combines word processing, spreadsheet, data base management, communications, and graphics applications in a single package.
- **Windowing Environment** Working closely with the operating system, a windowing environment allows you to divide your screen into a number of different boxes, or *windows*, and run a separate program in each one.
- **DOS Shell** A DOS shell is a program that enhances PC-DOS or MS-DOS, the operating system used with IBM and IBM-compatible microcomputers. Basically, it is an easy-to-use front-end to DOS that helps you execute commands and manage disk files.
- **Utilities** There are a host of small, specific programs called utilities that add handy features and functions to a particular operating system or application package. These include disk and file utilities, printer utilities, keyboard utilities, and desk accessories such as calculators, calendars, and address books.
- **On-Line References** Software to help you check your spelling, find a synonym, or look up a word's definition are all examples of on-line references.
- **Statistics and Math** Many programs exist for performing statistical analyses and helping solve mathematical equations.
- **Project Management** A project management package is software that helps you formally plan and control complex undertakings, such as the construction of a building, the development of a new product, or the installation of a large computer system.
- **Personal Finance and Taxes** Many programs exist for helping you manage your money and prepare your federal and state income tax returns.
- **Education** There is a wide range of programs for teaching skills and concepts, from learning the alphabet to designing physics experiments.

- **Entertainment** An amazing variety of microcomputer software exists for playing games, simulating cars and planes, and playing music.
- **Hypertext** A hypertext package is software that lets you store and retrieve all kinds of information in a nonsequential manner. In other words, you can randomly jump from topic to related topic, accessing any kind of information the computer can store, including text, graphics, audio, and video.
- **Expert System** An expert system is a computer program that contains a collection of facts and a list of rules for making inferences about those facts. Such software can use these facts and rules in a particular field to advise, analyze, categorize, diagnose, explain, identify, interpret, and teach.

Helpful Hints for Using a Microcomputer

Now that we've covered the general topics, let's go over a few specific details that can help prepare you for using a microcomputer.

Turning on the Computer

Sometimes, just turning on the computer can be an adventure. It seems that some manufacturers are fond of "hiding" the **power switch**. This has the practical purpose of making it difficult to turn off the computer by accident while in the middle of some critical task. Not being able to find the power switch, however, can make you feel lost before you even begin.

On the new IBM Personal System/2 computers, the power switch is a big red toggle right up front on the system unit. No problem here. On other computers, if the switch isn't immediately obvious up front, then it is probably on the right side of the system unit toward the rear. This is the case in IBM PCs, XTs, and ATs. Some models from other companies have the power switch mounted somewhere on the back side of the system unit or monitor.

Speaking of monitors, many color graphics displays have a separate power switch that must also be turned on, otherwise you will be looking at a permanently blank screen. The on/off switch is usually the top knob of three on the front of the monitor and is turned on by rotating it to the right. The other two knobs are the contrast and brightness controls, just like the ones on many television sets. If these three controls aren't right up front, they may be present as slightly protruding little disks located just under the bottom front edge of the monitor. Another possibility is the ever-popular back side of the monitor.

Operating the Printer

Like the system unit and monitor, the printer also has a power switch that must be turned on. This power switch is frequently positioned at the rear of the left or right side. In addition, there are at least three other buttons on most printers. Usually stationed on the top or front of the printer, these three buttons may be labeled On Line, Line Feed, and Form Feed. The **On Line** button is very important and is usually paired with an indicator light. When the On Line light is on, the printer is connected to and controlled by the computer, so that printing can occur. Make sure the On Line button is pressed so that the On Line light is on before attempting to print. The **Line Feed** and **Form Feed** buttons let you advance the paper in the printer, usually only when the printer is off line.

Caring for Floppy Disks

Although floppy disks are quite durable and can take quite a bit of punishment, there are a few guidelines you should follow in their handling:

1. Don't touch the exposed surfaces on 5¼-inch disks. Don't open the little metal door on 3½-inch disks.
2. Don't bend or fold 5¼-inch floppies.
3. Don't expose disks to extreme heat.
4. Keep 5¼-inch disks in their sleeves when not in use.
5. Don't write on 5¼-inch disks with pencils or hard point pens.
6. Keep your disks dry.
7. Don't expose disks to strong magnetic fields (keep them away from magnets and powerful motors).
8. Always try to keep at least one backup copy of all important disks.
9. Carefully insert and remove disks from disk drives. Wait until the drive's red access light is off before changing disks.

Conclusion

In this chapter of the *Software Guide*, you've learned what a microcomputer is, what it does, and what kinds of software are available. In addition, you've learned a few tips for turning on a microcomputer, operating a printer, and caring for floppy disks. This material sets the stage for the next chapter, in which you will complete lessons to teach you how to use PC-DOS and MS-DOS, the operating systems for IBM and IBM-compatible microcomputers.

Exercises

Multiple Choice

Choose the best selection to complete each statement.

_____ 1. A microcomputer is a computer in which the central processing unit consists of
  (a) a RAM chip.   (c) a microprocessor chip.
  (b) a ROM chip.   (d) a device controller chip.

_____ 2. A set of instructions that controls a computer's operation is
  (a) a program.   (c) input.
  (b) data.   (d) output.

_____ 3. The main circuit board of a computer is called the
  (a) expansion board.   (c) bus.
  (b) device controller.   (d) motherboard or system board.

_____ 4. IBM and IBM-compatible microcomputers use microprocessors from the
  (a) Motorola 68000 family.   (c) Zilog Z80 family.
  (b) Intel 8088 family.   (d) GTE G65SC816 family.

_____ 5. A byte is the amount of storage needed to hold a
  (a) single character.   (c) single line.
  (b) single page.   (d) single file.

6. Which of the following does NOT describe random access memory (RAM)?
   - (a) It is temporary storage.
   - (b) It loses its contents when the power is turned off.
   - (c) It is permanently encoded at the factory.
   - (d) It can be read and written over and over again.

7. The two most popular floppy disk sizes are
   - (a) 3½-inch and 8-inch.
   - (b) 5¼-inch and 8-inch.
   - (c) 3½-inch and 5¼-inch.
   - (d) 3-inch and 12-inch.

8. Which of the following types of display systems can present text and pictures on the screen, but in only a single color?
   - (a) monochrome text display
   - (b) monochrome graphics display
   - (c) color graphics display
   - (d) monochrome display adapter

9. Which of the following microcomputer keyboard keys is used to tell the computer to go ahead and process what was just typed?
   - (a) Enter or Return key
   - (b) Escape key
   - (c) Control key
   - (d) Function key

10. The most advanced and expensive type of printer in the following group is the
    - (a) dot-matrix printer.
    - (b) daisy-wheel printer.
    - (c) ink-jet printer.
    - (d) laser printer.

11. A set of programs that controls a computer's hardware and manages the use of software is called
    - (a) an operating system.
    - (b) a programming language.
    - (c) an application package.
    - (d) a data base management package.

12. Which of the following types of software lets you manipulate tables of numbers, text, and formulas?
    - (a) word processing package
    - (b) spreadsheet package
    - (c) data base management package
    - (d) operating system

13. Which of the following types of software lets you use a modem to transmit and receive programs and data over ordinary telephone lines?
    - (a) communications package
    - (b) graphics package
    - (c) desktop publishing package
    - (d) windowing package

14. Which of the following types of software lets you use a computer to record, analyze, and report business transactions?
    - (a) graphics package
    - (b) accounting package
    - (c) DOS shell
    - (d) utilities

15. Small, specific programs that add handy features and functions to a particular operating system or application package are called
    - (a) on-line references.
    - (b) hypertext programs.
    - (c) spreadsheets.
    - (d) utilities.

16. Which of the following types of software would be the best choice for maintaining a mailing list?
    - (a) word processing package
    - (b) spreadsheet package
    - (c) data base management package
    - (d) accounting package

17. Which of the following types of programs would you use to help plan and control the construction of a new office building?
    - (a) word processing package
    - (b) spreadsheet package
    - (c) integrated software package
    - (d) project management package

_____ 18. Which of the following types of software lets you store and retrieve all kinds of information in a nonsequential manner and then randomly jump from topic to related topic?
    (a) word processing package   (c) hypertext package
    (b) spreadsheet package   (d) expert system

_____ 19. Which printer button determines whether the printer is connected to and controlled by the computer?
    (a) Power   (c) Line Feed
    (b) On Line   (d) Form Feed

_____ 20. Which of the following should you NOT do to a floppy disk?
    (a) Keep it in its sleeve when not in use.   (c) Keep it near a magnet when not in use.
    (b) Keep it away from extreme heat.   (d) Keep it dry.

Fill-In

1. An _____ microcomputer works like a comparable IBM model and can run the same software.

2. At the lowest level, the basic operations of all computers can be summed up as input, _____, and output.

3. The _____ of a computer system is the electronic and mechanical equipment that make it work.

4. A microcomputer's motherboard contains the _____, which is a set of wires and connectors that link the CPU to memory and other computer components.

5. _____ is temporary storage for programs and data, which can be used and then overwritten by other programs and data. _____, on the other hand, is permanent storage encoded at the factory with frequently used programs and data that need never be changed.

6. Most microcomputers can be equipped with two basic types of disk drives: floppy disk drives and _____.

7. The number and size of a monitor's _____ determine its sharpness, or resolution.

8. The _____ is the display adapter that comes built onto the motherboards of high-end IBM Personal System/2 microcomputers.

9. Many microcomputers have an auxiliary input device known as a _____, which is a little box with one or more buttons that is glided across the table top.

10. On an IBM keyboard, the _____ Movement keys include Up Arrow, Down Arrow, Left Arrow, Right Arrow, Home, End, Page Up and Page Down.

11. _____ printers are by far the most popular type of microcomputer printer.

12. _____ is a general term that refers to any single program or group of programs.

13. BASIC, Pascal, C, FORTRAN, COBOL, and Ada are all examples of popular programming _____.

14. _____ software is the software that applies the computer to useful tasks such as helping you create documents, prepare a budget, or maintain a mailing list.

15. _____ packages let you use a computer to create all kinds of graphs, charts, maps, paintings, drawings, diagrams, slide shows, and presentations.

16. Combining the results of word processing and graphics software, _____ software lets you use a computer and laser printer to produce near typeset quality documents.

17. _____ software combines word processing, spreadsheet, data base management, communications, and graphics applications in a single package.

18. A _____ environment allows you to divide your screen into a number of different boxes and run a separate program in each one.

19. A _____ management package is software that helps you formally plan and control complex undertakings.

20. An _____ system is a computer program that contains a collection of facts and a list of rules for making inferences about those facts.

2

The PC-DOS Operating System

Learning Objectives

After reading this chapter, you should know how to do the following:

- Explain what a disk operating system is
- Explain why there are different versions of PC-DOS
- Boot PC-DOS with the computer turned off
- Boot PC-DOS with the computer turned on
- Obtain a directory listing of a disk's files
- Explain the structure of a PC-DOS file name
- Use the special PC-DOS keys
- Change the default disk drive
- Obtain a disk and memory status report
- Clear the display screen

- Format a diskette
- Format a system diskette
- Copy files
- Copy entire diskettes
- Change file names
- Erase files
- Display a text file on the screen
- Send a text file to the printer
- Run an application program
- Create and use DOS subdirectories
- Use DOS batch files

Introduction

An operating system is a set of programs that helps you use the hardware and software resources of a general-purpose computer. It's what you use to tell the computer to perform common tasks such as running application packages, managing disk storage, and controlling peripheral devices such as display screens and printers. In one sense, an operating system is like a toolbox that contains all kinds of utility programs to perform many of the little jobs that most users need. These utilities are like tools; some are used everyday by almost everyone, while others are more exotic and may only be used occasionally, even by experts.

A **disk operating system** (or **DOS**) is kept on a floppy or hard disk. When the computer system is turned on, some components of the operating system are loaded from disk into primary memory and remain there until the computer is shut off. These components, called **resident routines** or **internal commands**, are kept in memory because they are the most essential or the most frequently used parts of the operating system. The other components of a DOS are kept on disk and are temporarily loaded into memory only when they are needed or specifically requested. As a result, these latter commands are often called **transient routines** or **external commands**.

An important characteristic of a disk operating system is the abundance of utilities to deal with files that are stored on disks. A file, you'll recall, is just a collection of related data that is kept on a disk. Since most programs, text, and numerical data are kept in disk files, almost everything you do with computers involves working with files. Every computer user, therefore, must deal with an operating system to some extent. This chapter of the guide will teach you how to use the most popular disk operating system for IBM and IBM-compatible microcomputers.

PC-DOS and MS-DOS

PC-DOS, which stands for *Personal Computer Disk Operating System*, is by far the most popular operating system IBM offers for its microcomputers. It was written for IBM by Microsoft Corporation, which kept the right to also sell the same operating system itself under its own name, **MS-DOS**. Although there are some minor differences between PC-DOS and MS-DOS, from the average user's viewpoint they are virtually identical. The major distinction is that PC-DOS is generally used with IBM computers, and MS-DOS is used with the many compatible computers made by companies such as Compaq, AT&T, Tandy, and Zenith. From now on, everything we say about PC-DOS will also be true for MS-DOS, and so we'll just refer to both of them generically as DOS.

DOS Versions

Because computer technology changes so rapidly, an operating system like DOS is not a static entity. Operating systems must be constantly updated to accommodate new computer models and new capabilities for existing models. So far, there have been several official releases, or versions, of DOS. Although bugs have been worked out and improvements made over previous versions, the driving force behind each new release of DOS has been a new hardware capability, usually related to floppy or hard disk drives.

It's important to know which version of DOS you are using, because some hardware and software can only be used with more recent versions. Fortunately, each new version of DOS is **upwardly compatible** with former versions–that is, almost everything that worked with previous versions should work with the new version. So, you probably don't have to change the way you did things before unless you want to take advantage of the added capabilities of the new version. In fact, you usually don't have to buy the latest version of DOS each time a new release is issued. As long as the version you have works with your hardware and software, you can continue using it.

DOS versions are denoted by numbers such as 1.00, 2.10, and 3.30. The number to the left of the decimal point reflects a major classification; the numbers to the right represent more minor differences. The bigger the number, the more recent the version. Table 2.1 shows a summary of the DOS versions that have been released so far. Throughout this guide, we'll be using DOS 3.30 for all of our examples. Don't be concerned if you don't have the same version of DOS; everything we'll be covering will work for all versions 2.00 or newer.

Table 2.1

Version	Date	Hardware Support (Reason for New Version)
1.00	8/81	IBM PC single-sided floppy disk drive
1.10	5/82	IBM PC double-sided floppy disk drive
2.00	3/83	IBM XT 10 megabyte hard disk drive
2.10	10/83	IBM PCjr & Portable PC half-height floppy
3.00	8/84	IBM AT high-capacity floppy & hard disk
3.10	3/85	IBM AT network disks
3.20	12/85	IBM PC Convertible 3½-inch disk drive
3.30	3/87	IBM Personal System/2 disk drives
4.00	7/88	Hard disks larger than 35 megabytes

General Features of PC-DOS

PC-DOS provides many capabilities, both simple and complex. We'll be discussing some of its most used simple features, such as the following:

- **Booting Up with the Power Off** DOS can automatically load itself into memory when you turn the power on.
- **Booting Up with the Power On** DOS can be reloaded and reset without having to turn the power off and then on again.
- **Keeping Track of the Date and Time** Once you initially tell DOS the date and time, it will keep track of them until you turn the computer off or reboot.
- **Listing File Directories** You can instruct DOS to produce a directory of some or all of the files on a particular disk.
- **Using Special Keys** By pressing certain keys on the keyboard, you can tell DOS to cancel an input line, pause screen scrolling, cancel a command, print the screen, and echo input and output to the printer.
- **Changing the Default Drive** DOS lets you specify the disk drive it will assume when a drive designation isn't explicitly given.
- **Checking Disk and Memory Status** DOS can produce a report of useful information about a disk and primary memory.
- **Clearing the Screen** DOS lets you erase your display screen.
- **Formatting a Diskette** DOS lets you prepare a new diskette so that program and data files can be stored on it. It can also install itself on a new diskette if you tell it to do so.
- **Copying Files** DOS permits you to copy files onto the same disk or from one disk to another.
- **Copying Diskettes** DOS allows you to copy an entire diskette with a single command.
- **Changing File Names** DOS lets you choose new names for existing files.
- **Erasing Files** DOS allows you to delete unneeded files from a disk.
- **Displaying Text Files** You can have DOS display text files on your screen.
- **Printing Text Files** You can have DOS send text files to your printer.
- **Running Programs** You can tell DOS to run application programs such as dBASE III PLUS.
- **Using Subdirectories** You can create, use, and remove subdirectories, which are like separate little disks on a large disk.
- **Using Batch Files** You can create and execute collections of DOS commands stored in special text files called batch files.

Getting Started

Although DOS is a rich and powerful microcomputer operating system, you can quite easily learn its most commonly used features. For the most part, these features are invoked by issuing commands to DOS. A **command** is simply a word or mnemonic (memory aid) abbreviation entered at the keyboard that tells DOS to run a particular program. Once DOS has been initially loaded into memory, it's constantly on the lookout for these commands. In the following lessons you'll learn most of the DOS commands you're likely to need. You'll also be introduced to general concepts about the keyboard, display, disks, and disk drives that you'll be using in this and later parts. Wherever it's useful, figures will actually show you what you should see on your computer screen at a given point. These screen views will help you as you go through each lesson's steps.

DOS 3.30 comes on two floppy disks; one is labeled DOS Startup and the other is entitled DOS Operating. Previous versions of DOS also came on two disks, but these were labeled DOS and DOS Supplemental Programs. If you are using one of these earlier versions of DOS, you just need the DOS disk. If you are using a computer with a hard disk or one connected to a local area network, DOS may already be installed on it, but you can still use the DOS floppy disk or disks for the following lessons.

As you go through the lessons, you will be given instructions on what to type. In this text we'll use **bold** print to indicate what you're supposed to type. It doesn't matter whether you use uppercase or lowercase. DOS ignores case when processing commands.

Lesson 1: Booting DOS

The first thing that you must do is turn on your computer and load DOS into primary memory. This process is often called *booting DOS*, *loading DOS*, or simply *starting DOS*.

Step 1: Insert the DOS Disk

With the computer shut off, grasp the DOS 3.30 Startup disk (or DOS disk for previous versions) by the label and remove it from the sleeve (be careful not to touch the exposed parts around the oval slot and circular hole if it is a 5¼-inch disk). Hold the disk with the label side up and the oval slot pointing toward the computer. If your computer uses 3½-inch disks, hold the disk with the label up and the metal door pointed toward the computer. Insert the disk into the A drive and close the disk drive door. If your computer has two disk drives, side by side, the A drive is the one on the left. If it has two half-height drives arranged vertically, the A drive is the one on the top. If there is only one floppy drive, then it is the A drive.

Step 2: Turn the Computer On

If you have a color display, turn it on by twisting the top knob on the front panel to the right. If you have a monochrome display, you don't need to turn it on because its power cord is plugged into the computer. Turn on the computer by flipping up the big red switch, which is located right up front on the system unit of IBM Personal System/2 computers, or at the rear of the right side of the system unit on older IBM models. You should hear the cooling fan begin to whir.

Step 3: Watch the Display and Wait

Once the power is turned on, the computer goes through some self-tests to ensure that it is working properly. One of these tests checks out all of the primary memory installed. This could take a few seconds or several minutes depending upon how much memory the computer has. So, if nothing appears to be happening for a couple of minutes, don't be alarmed. After the power-on self-tests are complete, the computer will access drive A to see if the DOS disk is there. You should see the little red access light go on and hear the disk drive whir and click. Assuming the computer is in working order, the disk drive door is properly closed, and there is nothing wrong with the DOS disk, the DOS command processor and internal commands will be loaded into main memory and a message such as the following will appear on your display screen:

```
Current date is Tue  1-01-1980
Enter new date (mm-dd-yy): _
```

Step 4: Enter the Date and Time

Type today's date in the form of mm-dd-yy or mm/dd/yy. In other words, type in the month number, a dash or slash, the day of the month, another dash or slash, and the last two digits of the year. Now press the **Enter** key. After you have entered the date, a message like this will appear:

```
Current time is  0:00:36.90
Enter new time: _
```

Type the hour, a colon, and the minute, then press the **Enter** key. If it's afternoon, add twelve to the hour as in the military fashion. For example, if it's 2 P.M., enter **14:00**. You can enter the second and the hundreds of seconds if you happen to carry a stopwatch and feel so inclined. However, just the hour and minute are sufficient. After you do this, your screen should look something like the screen in Figure 2.1. The A> on the last line is called the **DOS prompt**. It indicates that disk drive A is your default drive and that the DOS command processor is patiently waiting for you to enter a command. The **default drive** is the disk drive that DOS assumes you want to use unless you specify otherwise.

Note: Many computers now have a battery-maintained clock/calendar that makes entering the date and time unnecessary. If the current date and time presented by DOS are correct, all you have to do is press the Enter key each time in response.

Figure 2.1   Booting Up DOS

```
Current date is Wed  1-01-1980
Enter new date (mm-dd-yy): 7-13-89
Current time is  0:00:36.26
Enter new time: 7:51


The IBM Personal Computer DOS
Version 3.30 (C)Copyright International Business Machines Corp 1981, 1987
              (C)Copyright Microsoft Corp 1981, 1986

A>_
```

Lesson 2: Rebooting DOS

Occasionally, something goes wrong in a program and the computer may seem to be "stuck." Or, after working with a program you may have to "reinitialize" the computer, or bring it back to the way it was when you first turned it on. You could, of course, just shut the computer off and boot it up as we outlined in Lesson 1. There's another way, however, to reboot the computer without shutting it off.

Step 1: Press Ctrl-Alt-Del

DOS has a special combination of keypresses that will reboot the computer without having to shut it off first. All you have to do is press the keys marked **Ctrl**, **Alt**, and **Del**, and hold them down at the same time for a moment.

Step 2: Watch the Display and Wait

In most cases, the screen will go blank, the computer will beep, and the disk drive will spin and blink its red access light just like it did when you first turned it on. If all this doesn't happen, a serious program error has probably overwritten a crucial part of DOS in memory and you will have to shut the computer off and boot it up as you did in Lesson 1. If all is well, DOS will again ask you to supply the date and time.

Step 3: Enter the Date and Time

After you enter the date and time as you did in Lesson 1, DOS will once again display its copyright message and the system prompt, as shown in Figure 2.1.

Lesson 3: Listing a Disk File Directory

As we mentioned before, programs, data, and text are kept on disks in files. Every file has a name, size, creation date, and creation time associated with it. DOS can display this information for you if you use the directory command.

Step 1: Enter the Directory Command

At the DOS prompt, type in the letters **dir** and press the **Enter** key. As with all DOS commands, it doesn't matter if you use uppercase or lowercase letters. DIR is is the abbreviation for the DOS directory command that will list the directory of the default disk on your display screen. Remember that the default disk is the one in the disk drive that DOS assumes you are currently working on, and its letter is indicated by the DOS prompt. Right now, your default disk drive should be A, so the DIR command will list the file names, sizes, and creation dates and times for all the files on the floppy disk in drive A. Figure 2.2 shows what the screen looks like when it stops scrolling.

Figure 2.2   Listing a Directory

```
COMMAND   COM    25307   3-17-87   12:00p
ANSI      SYS     1678   3-17-87   12:00p
COUNTRY   SYS    11285   3-17-87   12:00p
DISPLAY   SYS    11290   3-17-87   12:00p
DRIVER    SYS     1196   3-17-87   12:00p
FASTOPEN  EXE     3919   3-17-87   12:00p
FDISK     COM    48216   3-18-87   12:00p
FORMAT    COM    11616   3-18-87   12:00p
KEYB      COM     9056   3-17-87   12:00p
KEYBOARD  SYS    19766   3-17-87   12:00p
MODE      COM    15487   3-17-87   12:00p
NLSFUNC   EXE     3060   3-17-87   12:00p
PRINTER   SYS    13590   3-17-87   12:00p
REPLACE   EXE    11775   3-17-87   12:00p
SELECT    COM     4163   3-17-87   12:00p
SYS       COM     4766   3-17-87   12:00p
VDISK     SYS     3455   3-17-87   12:00p
XCOPY     EXE    11247   3-17-87   12:00p
EGA       CPI    49065   3-18-87   12:00p
LCD       CPI    10752   3-17-87   12:00p
4201      CPI    17089   3-18-87   12:00p
5202      CPI      459   3-17-87   12:00p
       22 File(s)        9216 bytes free

A>_
```

This is the directory of the PC-DOS 3.30 DOS Startup floppy disk. (If you are using a different version of DOS, the directory will be somewhat different.) Listed are the names, sizes, and creation dates and times of all the files on the DOS Startup disk. Notice that each file's name has two parts: a **primary file name**, which can be up to eight characters long, and a three-letter **extension**. We'll have more to say about this file name format later in this lesson. The number to the immediate right of each file's name is its size in bytes. A byte, you'll recall, is the amount of storage needed to hold a single character. Finally, listed with each file is the date and time it was created or last changed. So, for example, the file FORMAT.COM is made up of 11,616 bytes and was created at 12:00 P.M. on March 18, 1987.

At the very bottom of the listing, DOS informs you that there are 22 files in the directory and 9,216 bytes of empty room left on the disk. As you can imagine, it's pretty important to be able to see what's on a disk and how much room is left. For this reason, DIR is one of most frequently used DOS commands.

Incidentally, most of the files that you see in this directory listing with an extension of COM or EXE are external commands or transient routines of DOS. These are programs that reside on the DOS disk until you specifically call them up. In contrast, the DIR command is an internal command or resident routine. It too is a component program of DOS, but because it's used so frequently it's loaded into memory when DOS is booted and it's kept there. This means that DIR is not stored by itself in a separate file on the DOS disk; once you've booted up, you don't need the DOS disk in drive A to use the directory command.

Step 2: Examine Another Disk's Directory

The DIR command can also be used to list the directory of a disk in a drive other than the current default drive. You can do this by specifying the disk drive designation after typing dir. For example, to list the directory of a disk in drive B, you could enter this command:

dir b:

The **b:** is the designation for the B disk drive. If you have a computer with two floppy drives, remove the DOS disk from drive A, insert it into drive B, close the door, and enter **dir b:**. You should see the same directory listing you saw in Step 1 of this lesson. After you're done looking at the directory of drive B, make sure to put the DOS disk back into drive A.

If your computer has a hard disk drive and no second floppy drive, try entering **dir c:**. You should see some kind of directory listing, though it will probably be different from the one in Figure 2.2. This difference exists because many additional files are most likely stored on your hard disk. Note that the hard disk is usually referred to as the C drive regardless of whether a B floppy drive is installed.

Step 3: Look For a Specific File

Frequently, you'd like to be able to check if a particular file is on a disk without having to look at the entire directory. The DIR command can do this for you if you give it the name of the file you're looking for. All you have to do is enter the name of the file after typing dir. Then DOS either lists an abbreviated directory with only that file in it or tells you the file is not there. For example, enter this command:

> **dir a:format.com**

Figure 2.3 shows what you should see on your screen.

DOS File Names This is a good time to digress a bit and discuss DOS file names in more detail. First of all, notice that each file in the directory you listed has a unique name. No two files in the same directory can have the same name because DOS wouldn't be able to tell them apart. Two files on different disks, however, can have the same name. As we mentioned before, a file's full name can consist of

Figure 2.3   Looking for a Specific File

```
A>dir a:format.com

  Volume in drive A has no label
  Directory of  A:\

FORMAT   COM    11616   3-18-87  12:00p
         1 File(s)        9216 bytes free

A>_
```

two parts: a primary filename and an optional extension. The first part, or **file name** as IBM calls it, can be from one to eight characters long. It can include any of the characters you see on the keyboard except for the following, which are considered invalid in file names:

. " / \ [ ] : | < > + = ; ,

The second part, an optional short name, is called an **extension**. It is separated from the primary filename by a period and has from one to three characters in it. These characters also can be any of the keyboard characters except those invalid ones we just listed. If a file's name does have an extension, you must use both parts when telling DOS to do something with that file. Extensions are most often used to further classify files. For example, here are some of the more common file name extensions along with the types of files they usually designate:

.COM DOS external command files and other programs
.EXE Executable program files
.SYS DOS system configuration and device driver files
.BAT DOS batch files
.BAS BASIC language source code files
.PAS Pascal language source code files
.FOR FORTRAN language source code files
.ASM Assembly language source code files
.TXT Ordinary text files
.ASC ASCII files
.DOC Document files for some word processing programs
.WKS Lotus 1-2-3 Release 1A worksheet files
.WK1 Lotus 1-2-3 Release 2 and 2.01 worksheet files
.DBF dBASE III PLUS data base files

Finally, a file name can be prefaced with the designation of the disk drive that it's on. For example, A:FORMAT.COM is the specification for the file containing the FORMAT command on the DOS disk in drive A. Note that the colon must be used to separate the disk drive letter from the filename.

Step 4: Look for a Specific Group of Files

Not only can the DIR command find a single file on a disk, it can also be used to list a group of files if their names have some characters in common. This is possible through the use of the DOS global filename characters, * and ?. These characters can be included in a filename or extension to give you greater flexibility in designating DOS files. The * character can be used in a file specification to symbolize any character or group of characters. For example, *.SYS means "any file with an extension of SYS." The ? character is used to symbolize any single character. For example, MO?E.COM means "any file that has an extension of COM and a four-letter filename beginning with MO and ending with an E." Both global file name characters can be used together in the same specification, too. For example, ????.* means "any file with at most four characters in its first part." Try these examples yourself:

dir *.sys
dir mo?e.com
dir ????.*

Figure 2.4 shows what you should see on your screen after entering the command **dir *.sys.**

**Figure 2.4   Looking for a
Group of Files**

```
A>dir *.sys

 Volume in drive A has no label
 Directory of  A:\

ANSI     SYS     1678   3-17-87  12:00p
COUNTRY  SYS    11285   3-17-87  12:00p
DISPLAY  SYS    11290   3-17-87  12:00p
DRIVER   SYS     1196   3-17-87  12:00p
KEYBOARD SYS    19766   3-17-87  12:00p
PRINTER  SYS    13590   3-17-87  12:00p
VDISK    SYS     3455   3-17-87  12:00p
        7 File(s)       9216 bytes free

A>_
```

Lesson 4: Using Special DOS Keys

Like most software, DOS assigns special meanings to certain keys and combinations of keypresses. You've already learned some of these. For example, you know that you must press the Enter key after typing in a command. This tells DOS to go ahead and process that command. The Backspace key can be used to correct typing errors on a line before the Enter key has been pressed. Finally, you learned in Lesson 2 that pressing the Control (Ctrl), Alternate (Alt), and Delete (Del) keys all at the same time will reboot DOS without having to shut off and then turn the power back on. Let's explore some of the other keys DOS uses.

Step 1: Press the Escape Key to Cancel a Line

As you've probably already discovered, it's pretty easy to make typing mistakes when using a keyboard. If the command you're typing is short, and you haven't pressed the Enter key yet, the easiest way to fix a mistake is to backspace over it and retype it. If the command is long, or if you really messed up, you can cancel the entire line you just typed and start all over again. To do this, just press the Escape (Esc) key. For example, type the following line at the DOS prompt (but don't press the Enter key):

This line is really messed up!

Let's say what you really meant to type in was **dir**, and you realized your mistake before you pressed the Enter key. Just press **Escape** to cancel this line. When you do this, DOS will display a / (slash) after the exclamation point to signal that this line has been canceled and it will skip down to the next line so you can start over again. Enter **dir** and you'll see the familiar DOS directory again.

Step 2: Press Ctrl-Num Lock to Pause Screen Scrolling

As you watch the DOS directory scroll by on the screen, notice that the first part of it disappears off the top. Sometimes, information scrolls by before you get a chance to read it all. It would be nice if you could temporarily stop the screen so that you wouldn't have to take speed reading lessons to use the computer. Fortunately, DOS can accomplish this pause for you if you hold down the Control key and press the Num Lock key. On the newer IBM Enhanced style keyboards, you have to press the Pause key instead of Ctrl-Num Lock. In either case, this action will immediately pause any screen that is scrolling by. To resume scrolling, just press any key (except a Shift, Lock, Ctrl, or Alt key). Enter **dir** and press **Ctrl-Num Lock** or the **Pause** key. Figure 2.5 shows what can happen. You can pause and resume scrolling as many times as you wish.

Figure 2.5   Pausing Screen Scrolling

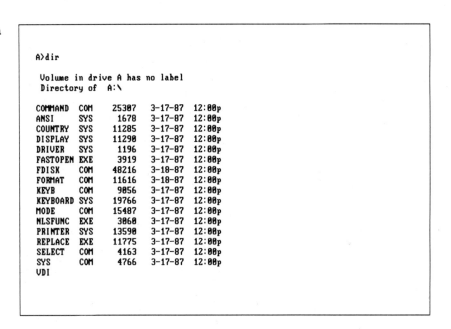

```
A>dir

   Volume in drive A has no label
   Directory of  A:\

COMMAND   COM     25307   3-17-87   12:00p
ANSI      SYS      1678   3-17-87   12:00p
COUNTRY   SYS     11285   3-17-87   12:00p
DISPLAY   SYS     11290   3-17-87   12:00p
DRIVER    SYS      1196   3-17-87   12:00p
FASTOPEN  EXE      3919   3-17-87   12:00p
FDISK     COM     48216   3-18-87   12:00p
FORMAT    COM     11616   3-18-87   12:00p
KEYB      COM      9056   3-17-87   12:00p
KEYBOARD  SYS     19766   3-17-87   12:00p
MODE      COM     15487   3-17-87   12:00p
NLSFUNC   EXE      3060   3-17-87   12:00p
PRINTER   SYS     13590   3-17-87   12:00p
REPLACE   EXE     11775   3-17-87   12:00p
SELECT    COM      4163   3-17-87   12:00p
SYS       COM      4766   3-17-87   12:00p
VDI
```

Step 3: Press Ctrl-Break to Cancel a Command

Let's say that you've entered **dir** by mistake and you don't want to wait for the whole directory to scroll by on the screen. Or perhaps you've seen enough and you just want to stop it. You can cancel a DOS command by pressing the Control and Break keys at the same time. This action stops a command from finishing its job normally. In many cases, Ctrl-Break will also terminate programs other than just DOS commands.

Enter **dir** and press **Ctrl-Break** to terminate the directory command before it would normally finish. Figure 2.6 shows how this might appear on your screen. The ^C signifies a Ctrl-C character which has canceled the command.

On IBM PC and AT style keyboards, the Break key is right next to the Num Lock key and it's also labeled Scroll Lock. On the newer IBM Enhanced style keyboards, the Break key is the same as the Pause key. On all types of keyboards, you can also cancel a command by holding down the Control key and typing a C. Note that Ctrl-Break (or Ctrl-C) is different from the Escape key. Escape will cancel a

Figure 2.6   Canceling a Command

```
A>dir

 Volume in drive A has no label
 Directory of  A:\

COMMAND  COM   25307   3-17-87  12:00p
ANSI     SYS    1678   3-17-87  12:00p
COUNTRY  SYS   11285   3-17-87  12:00p
DISPLAY  SYS   11290   3-17-87  12:00p
DRIVER   SYS    1196   3-17-87  12:00p
FASTOPEN EXE    3919   3-17-87  12:00p
FDISK    COM   48216   3-18-87  12:00p
FORMAT   COM    ^C

A>_
```

line typed in at the DOS prompt before the Enter key has been pressed. Ctrl-Break cancels a command after the Enter key has been pressed and the command is already executing.

Step 4: Press Shift-PrtSc to Print the Screen

Frequently there's a sequence of commands or some information on the screen that you'd like to save. If you have a printer connected to your computer, DOS can produce a hard copy of everything that's currently on the display screen. On IBM PC and AT style keyboards, you press one of the shift keys along with the key marked PrtSc (Print Screen). On the newer IBM Enhanced style keyboards, you simply press the key labeled Print Screen. If you don't have a printer, you'll just have to take our word for it; if you have a printer, make sure it's turned on and press **Shift-PrtSc** or press the **Print Screen** key. You should get a copy of what's on your screen right now.

Step 5: Press Ctrl-PrtSc to Echo to the Printer

Notice that the printout you got from the previous step contains only one screen of text. This output would be less than desirable if you wanted a hard copy of the entire DOS directory because the whole directory doesn't fit on a single screen at once. Pressing Ctrl-PrtSc (or Ctrl-Print Screen on the Enhanced style keyboards), however, will cause whatever you type and the computer's responses to be displayed both on the screen and sent to the printer. This echoing will continue until you press Ctrl-PrtSc again. So, you could, for example, get a hard copy of your entire computer session.

To get a hard copy of the DOS disk directory, press **Ctrl-PrtSc** and then enter **dir**. You should see the directory information being displayed on the screen a bit slower as it is also being sent to the printer. When it's done and you get the DOS prompt again, press **Ctrl-PrtSc** to turn off printer echoing.

Lesson 5:   Changing the Default Disk Drive

So far, you've been doing all your work on the A disk drive. The DOS prompt has been A>, which indicates that drive A is your current default disk drive. Thus, whenever you enter a command that doesn't explicitly specify a particular disk drive, the A drive is assumed. For example, when you enter **dir**, you get a directory of the disk in the default drive, which is currently drive A. If your computer has more than one disk drive, and most IBMs and IBM-compatibles do, you may sometime want to change your default drive from A to B, or to C if you have a hard disk. DOS makes it easy to take advantage of this feature, which is also called *switching drives*.

Step 1:   Enter the Designation of the New Default Drive

If you have a computer with two floppy drives, you can change your default drive from A to B by typing **b:** and pressing the **Enter** key. If you have a computer with a hard disk, you can change your default drive from A to the hard disk by typing **c:** and pressing the **Enter** key. As soon as you do this, DOS responds with a new prompt, which indicates the new default drive. So, if you have two floppy drives and you enter **b:**, DOS responds with B> as the new prompt. If you have a hard disk and you enter **c:**, DOS responds with C> as the new prompt.

Step 2:   Use the New Default Drive

If you have two floppy drives, remove the DOS disk from drive A and put it into the B drive and close the door. Now enter a DIR command, such as **dir *.sys.** The directory listing you get now will be of the new default drive, B or C (see Figure 2.7). Although this might not seem terribly exciting at the moment, being able to change the default drive easily enables you to make full use of all of your installed disk drives. As you become more proficient with DOS and application packages, you'll find yourself switching default disk drives often. For example, on systems with two floppy drives, you may leave the DOS disk in drive A and a disk containing a particular application program in drive B. Then, after booting up, you would switch to drive B to run your application program.

Figure 2.7   Changing the Default Disk Drive

```
A>b:

B>dir *.sys

 Volume in drive B has no label
 Directory of  B:\

ANSI     SYS     1678    3-17-87   12:00p
COUNTRY  SYS    11285    3-17-87   12:00p
DISPLAY  SYS    11290    3-17-87   12:00p
DRIVER   SYS     1196    3-17-87   12:00p
KEYBOARD SYS    19766    3-17-87   12:00p
PRINTER  SYS    13590    3-17-87   12:00p
VDISK    SYS     3455    3-17-87   12:00p
        7 File(s)     9216 bytes free

B>a:

A>_
```

Step 3: Switch Back to Disk Drive A

Enter **a:** to change the default directory back to the A drive. If you put the DOS disk in drive B, remove it and put it back into the A drive.

Lesson 6: Checking Disk and Memory Status

You've already learned how to use the DIR command to examine the contents of a disk's directory. In addition to this, DOS provides a command that can display a status report about a disk and the memory installed in your computer. This report contains some interesting and useful information. With DOS 3.30, this command is on the DOS Operating disk. If you're using DOS 3.30, take the DOS Startup disk out of drive A and replace it with the DOS Operating disk. If you're using a previous version of DOS, you don't need to change disks.

Step 1: Enter CHKDSK

With the appropriate disk in drive A, type **chkdsk** and press the **Enter** key. This will invoke the DOS check disk command and produces a report on your screen that looks something like the Figure 2.8. If you're not using DOS version 3.30 or if your computer has more or less than 512 kilobytes (512K) of primary memory, the numbers in your report will be different.

Step 2: Examine the Status Report

This status report tells you several useful things. It tells you that the total capacity of the disk currently in the default drive is 362,496 bytes (equivalent to about 100 pages of text). Admittedly, the "0 bytes in 1 hidden files" statement doesn't make much sense. You can simply ignore it in this case. The hidden files mentioned in the report are parts of DOS that are kept on the disk, but do not appear in the disk

Figure 2.8   The CHKDSK Report

```
A>chkdsk

    362496 bytes total disk space
     53248 bytes in 3 hidden files
    300032 bytes in 22 user files
      9216 bytes available on disk

    524288 bytes total memory
    399984 bytes free

A>_
```

directory. These files contain important DOS programs that are kept hidden from you so that you don't rename, change, or delete them. The CHKDSK report then tells you that there are 31 ordinary user files on the disk and that they occupy 307,200 bytes of space. That leaves 55,296 bytes of empty space still on the disk. Finally, CHKDSK tells you that 524,288 bytes (or 512K) of primary memory are installed in this computer and that 472,064 bytes of these are free for use by application programs. The difference between these latter two figures, 52,224 bytes, is the amount of primary memory taken up by the parts of DOS that remain resident–the command processor and the internal commands.

Lesson 7: Clearing the Screen

By now, you've probably accumulated quite a collection of commands and directory listings on your screen. Although this does no harm, it can be a bit distracting. Or, perhaps you want to type a sequence of commands and then do a print screen, and you would like to start off with a clean slate. Don't worry, it's easy to tell DOS to erase the screen.

Step 1: Enter CLS

To clear the screen, simply type **cls** and press the **Enter** key. DOS will then erase everything from the screen and start you off again with the system prompt on the first line in the upper left corner.

Lesson 8: Formatting a Diskette

Before a new floppy disk can be used to store programs and data files, it must undergo an initial preparation known as formatting. This preparation is not done at the factory, so you must do it with your own computer for each brand new diskette you're going to use. Although you usually format a new diskette only once, you can format a previously formatted disk in order to clear it off completely. Formatting a floppy basically consists of the following procedures:

- Checking the diskette for bad spots
- Wiping out any information that might be on the diskette
- Building a directory that will hold information about the files that will be on the diskette
- Marking off the empty space into equal-sized chunks called **sectors**
- Copying DOS onto the diskette if specified to do so

The DOS FORMAT command can automatically do all this for you.

Step 1: Get a Floppy Disk to Format

For this lesson you'll need a new floppy disk or a previously used disk that can be completely erased. If you are going to format a diskette that's not new, double check to make sure it doesn't have any programs or data files on it that you want to keep. Formatting a disk erases everything that's on it.

If it is a used 5¼-inch diskette, also make sure that it doesn't have a write-protect tab on it. If you hold the diskette right side up with your thumb on the label, you should be able to see a little square notch cut into it on the left edge. If this notch is not covered up, then it's not write-protected and it's all right to use. If the diskette has a gummed tab covering the notch, then remove the tab. If the diskette has no notch, then it's permanently write-protected and you'll have to use another diskette.

Step 2: Put the DOS Startup Disk in A and the New Disk in B

On a computer with two floppy disk drives, make sure the DOS Startup disk is in drive A. Put the disk you want to format into drive B and close both doors. If your computer has only one floppy disk drive, just make sure the DOS Startup disk is in it. The FORMAT command will tell you when to put the new diskette in.

Step 3: Enter the FORMAT Command

On a computer with two floppy disk drives, type **format b:** and press the **Enter** key. On a computer with just one floppy drive, type **format a:** and press the **Enter** key. The FORMAT command will then tell you to insert the new diskette into drive B (for two-floppy systems) or drive A (for single-floppy systems). Insert the disk as indicated, and press the **Enter** key.

Step 4: Wait for FORMAT to Finish

The formatting procedure will take a minute or so, during which you should see the disk drive access light go on. When the procedure is done, the FORMAT command will tell you how much room is on the disk and if it contained any bad sectors. The command will then ask you if you want to format another diskette and you can enter **n** for no. You'll then get the DOS prompt back again. When you're done, your screen should look something Figure 2.9.

Figure 2.9 shows you that there are 362,496 bytes of total disk space and all of that space is available for files. In other words, no bad areas were detected. If there were any bad sectors found on the disk, less space would be available. DOS would mark these sectors as unusable and prevent them from being used to store files.

Figure 2.9   Formatting a Diskette

```
A>format b:
Insert new diskette for drive B:
and strike ENTER when ready

Format complete

   362496 bytes total disk space
   362496 bytes available on disk

Format another (Y/N)?n
A>_
```

Lesson 9: Formatting a System Diskette

The diskette you've just formatted can now be used to store programs and data files. It cannot, however, be used to boot the computer because it does not have DOS installed on it. If you want to format a diskette so that DOS is installed, the procedure is slightly different.

Step 1: Use the /S Parameter

Many DOS commands can be given options that specify a slightly different way of performing their tasks. The FORMAT command, for example, can be instructed to install the operating system on the disk it's preparing. To do this, simply type /s after the drive designator of the disk to format. The /s tells FORMAT to put the DOS internal commands and the command processor on the disk being formatted. You can try this out by reformatting the disk you just formatted as we outlined in Lesson 8. This time, however, enter this command:

format b:/s

Step 2: Examine the Disk's Directory

Now the FORMAT command will tell you that the system was transferred and that 78,848 bytes were used by the operating system. Only 283,648 bytes are left available on the disk. Enter **dir b:**. Your screen should look like Figure 2.10. Notice that only the file COMMAND.COM is on the new system disk. It does not contain any of the external command files that are on the DOS disk. So, although you could boot up with this new disk, and you could execute internal commands such as DIR, you could not use any external commands such as CHKDSK or FORMAT unless you somehow copied their command files onto it.

Figure 2.10   Formatting a System Diskette

```
A>format b:/s
Insert new diskette for drive B:
and strike ENTER when ready

Format complete
System transferred

    362496 bytes total disk space
    78848 bytes used by system
    283648 bytes available on disk

Format another (Y/N)?n
A>dir b:

 Volume in drive B has no label
 Directory of  B:\

COMMAND  COM   25307   3-17-87  12:00p
        1 File(s)    283648 bytes free

A>_
```

Lesson 10: Copying Files

Once a diskette has been formatted, it can be used to store program and data files. But how do you get files onto the new diskette? One way is by using the DOS COPY command. The COPY command can be used to duplicate one or more files on the same or on different diskettes. As a very versatile command, COPY can be used in several different ways.

Step 1: Copy a Single File (the Long Way)

Let's use the COPY command to copy a single file from the DOS Startup disk onto your newly formatted disk. For starters, we'll do it the longhand way and then we'll show you the shortcut. To copy the file FORMAT.COM from the DOS Startup disk onto your new disk, first make sure the DOS Startup disk is in drive A and the new disk is in drive B. Then enter this command:

copy a:format.com b:format.com

The first file name is the *source*, or what you're copying from–the file FORMAT.COM on the disk in drive A. The second file name is the *target*, or what you're copying to–a file named FORMAT.COM on the disk in drive B. After you do this, DOS will tell you that one file was copied. If you enter **dir b:** you should see the file FORMAT.COM in the directory of the disk in drive B. Figure 2.11 shows what you should see on your screen.

Figure 2.11   Copy a File

```
A>copy a:format.com b:format.com
        1 File(s) copied

A>dir b:

 Volume in drive B has no label
 Directory of  B:\

COMMAND  COM    25307   3-17-87   12:00p
FORMAT   COM    11616   3-18-87   12:00p
        2 File(s)    271360 bytes free

A>_
```

Step 2: Copy a Single File (the Short Way)

In most cases, if you omit certain information, DOS will assume the default values. For example, if you don't supply a disk drive designation in front of a filename, DOS will assume that you mean the default drive. Similarly, if you don't specify a name for the target file, the COPY command will assume that it is to use the same name as the source. This assumption will work as long as the source and the target

files are on different disks. So, another way to copy FORMAT.COM would be to
enter this command:

copy format.com b:

This command means copy the file FORMAT.COM on the disk in the default drive
to the disk in drive B and give it the same name. Try this shorter command. Realize, however, that you will be copying the FORMAT.COM on drive A to the
FORMAT.COM that already exists on drive B from our first copy operation. If you
choose a name that already exists as the target, DOS will happily copy over it, de-
stroying whatever was in that file before. Since we're copying the exact same file,
there's no problem here. As a rule, however, you should be very careful about the
name you choose for a target file. If it already exists on the disk you're copying to,
the original version will be overwritten.

Step 3: Copy a Group of Files

By using the global file name characters * and ? we introduced in Lesson 3, you
can copy several files all at once with a single COPY command. For example, with
the DOS Startup disk in drive A and your newly formatted disk in drive B, enter
this command:

copy *.* b:

This will copy every single file on the disk in the default drive to the disk in drive
B. Figure 2.12 shows what your screen should look like when this command is
completed.

Step 4: Copy a File to the Same Disk

All the examples we've covered so far have copied files from one disk to another.
Also, the target file names have all been the same as the source file names. This
arrangement, however, needn't always be so. The COPY command can be used to
duplicate a file on the same disk. The only catch is that you have to choose a different name for the target. Remember that no two files in the same directory can
have the same name.

Figure 2.12 Copying a Group of Files

```
COMMAND.COM
ANSI.SYS
COUNTRY.SYS
DISPLAY.SYS
DRIVER.SYS
FASTOPEN.EXE
FDISK.COM
FORMAT.COM
KEYB.COM
KEYBOARD.SYS
MODE.COM
NLSFUNC.EXE
PRINTER.SYS
REPLACE.EXE
SELECT.COM
SYS.COM
VDISK.SYS
XCOPY.EXE
EGA.CPI
LCD.CPI
4201.CPI
5202.CPI
        22 File(s) copied

A>_
```

One common reason for duplicating a file on the same disk with a different name is for backup purposes. Let's say that you are going to change an existing file. If that file is especially important, you might want to keep a copy of the original version before you change it. One of the great advantages of using computers is the ease with which they can copy files. So, before you change your file, make a copy of it and give the copy a different name. As an example, with your DOS disk in drive A and your newly formatted disk in drive B, enter this command:

copy b:format.com b:format.bak

This will create a copy of the FORMAT.COM file on the disk in drive B and it will be named FORMAT.BAK (BAK for backup). Now you can go ahead and make your modifications, safe in the knowledge that you've retained a copy of the original file.

Lesson 11: Copying an Entire Diskette

DOS has a more specific copy command that lets you copy an entire diskette all at once. What's more, this command automatically formats the target diskette if it's new. When you need an exact copy of an entire diskette, the DISKCOPY command can do the trick. DISKCOPY only works, however, if the source and target are the same type of disk. For instance, you cannot use the DISKCOPY command to duplicate the contents of a 5¼-inch diskette on a 3½-inch diskette. To see how the DISKCOPY command does work, let's make an exact copy of our DOS Startup diskette on the new diskette we've been working with.

Step 1: Put the DOS Operating Disk in Drive A

With DOS 3.30, DISKCOPY is an external command stored on the DOS Operating disk. So, the first step is to put the DOS Operating disk into drive A.

Step 2: Issue the DISKCOPY Command

If your computer has two identical floppy disk drives, enter this command:

diskcopy a: b:

If your computer has only one floppy drive or two drives that are of different types, such as a 5¼-inch drive and a 3½-inch drive, enter this command instead:

diskcopy a: a:

Step 3: Follow the Directions

The DISKCOPY command will tell you which drive to put your source and target diskettes into and when to do so. Remember: the DOS Startup diskette is the source, and the new diskette is the target. If your machine has only one floppy drive, you may have to swap the source and target diskettes in drive A several times. When it's done, DISKCOPY will ask you if you want to copy another diskette and you can enter **n** for no. If you have two floppy drives, Figure 2.13 shows what you should see on your screen when DISKCOPY is done.

**Figure 2.13 Copying an
Entire Diskette**

```
A>diskcopy a: b:

Insert SOURCE diskette in drive A:

Insert TARGET diskette in drive B:

Press any key when ready . . .

Copying 40 tracks
9 Sectors/Track, 2 Side(s)


Copy another diskette (Y/N)?n


A>_
```

DISKCOPY is a very useful command for making backup copies of especially important diskettes. In fact, the documentation that comes with many software packages suggests that you use the DISKCOPY command to duplicate all of your original diskettes as soon as you get them. Furthermore, they say that you should put the originals away for safekeeping and only use your copies. Then, if you should accidentally erase something or if a diskette you use daily should become damaged or wear out, you would still have your original diskettes from which to make additional copies. These are good suggestions, and DISKCOPY will work fine as long as your software is not copy-protected.

Lesson 12: Changing File Names

When a file is originally created, the name it's given isn't set in stone; DOS lets you change file names very easily. Perhaps you've thought up a more appropriate name, or you want to abbreviate a long name. Another reason to change a file name is that you want to copy a file onto a disk that already has a file of the same name. If you don't change the name of the file already on the disk, copying a new file of the same name onto the disk will destroy the original file's contents. The DOS RENAME command allows you to change the names of one or more files.

Step 1: Rename a Single File

Changing a single file's name is quite easy. Just type rename (or its abbreviation, ren), followed by the file name you want to change, and then the new name that file is to have. For example, put the copy of the DOS Startup disk you made in Lesson 11 in drive A and enter this command:

rename format.com format.bak

Now enter this command to see what you've done:

dir format.*

Your screen should look like Figure 2.14. The directory shows that you've successfully changed the name of FORMAT.COM to FORMAT.BAK. This procedure would be very useful if you wanted to copy a new version of the FORMAT.COM file to your disk, yet still keep a copy of the original version. Since the backup version is safely stored as FORMAT.BAK, you could now copy a new FORMAT.COM onto your disk.

Figure 2.14   Renaming a File

```
A>rename format.com format.bak

A>dir format.*

 Volume in drive A has no label
 Directory of  A:\

FORMAT   BAK    11616   3-18-87  12:00p
        1 File(s)       9216 bytes free

A>_
```

Before you go on, change FORMAT.BAK back to FORMAT.COM so that the DOS Startup disk copy is like it was before. This time, however, try using the abbreviated form of the RENAME command:

ren format.bak format.com

Step 2: Rename Several Files at Once

By using the global file name characters * and ?, you can rename several files at once. For example, with a single command you could rename each file on your DOS Startup disk copy with an extension of EXE, and give it an extension of BAK. Try entering this command:

ren *.exe *.bak

Now enter this directory command to see what you've done:

dir *.bak

Your screen should look like Figure 2.15. There are now no files on your disk with EXE extensions. They all have BAK extensions instead. Before you go on, change them all back to the way they were with this command:

ren *.bak *.exe

Figure 2.15 Renaming a Group of Files

```
A>ren *.exe *.bak

A>dir *.bak

 Volume in drive A has no label
 Directory of  A:\

FASTOPEN BAK     3919   3-17-87  12:00p
NLSFUNC  BAK     3060   3-17-87  12:00p
REPLACE  BAK    11775   3-17-87  12:00p
XCOPY    BAK    11247   3-17-87  12:00p
        4 File(s)     9216 bytes free

A>_
```

Lesson 13: Erasing Files

Just as you accumulate old memos, notes, letters, and other scraps of this or that on your desk, disks can also become cluttered with unneeded files. Occasionally, it's necessary to clean up a bit and discard those items that you know you no longer need. Once you throw something away, however, it may be difficult or even impossible to get it back again. Be careful, therefore, to discard only files you're sure you can't use anymore. DOS makes it very easy to erase files, but it has no provision to unerase, or restore, them. Use the DOS ERASE command with caution.

Step 1: Erase a Single File

To erase a single file, just type in **erase** or **del** (for delete) and follow it with the name of the file you want to erase. Put your DOS Startup disk copy in drive A. Because it is a copy and you know that everything on it is also on the original DOS Startup disk, you can safely erase files. Nevertheless, we want to emphasize caution again. Data and programs are most frequently lost as the result of an accidentally or carelessly entered ERASE command than from any other cause. The original 5¼-inch disks that come with PC-DOS when you purchase it from IBM are permanently write-protected. They have no open square notches on the left edge. This means that you cannot delete any files from them with the ERASE command. The copy of the DOS disk you made in Lesson 11, however, is not write-protected, so you can erase files from it. Again make sure that your DOS Startup disk copy is in drive A, and enter this command to erase the FORMAT.COM file:

erase format.com

Now enter this directory command to see what you've done:

dir format.com

The file is now gone, so your screen should look like Figure 2.16.

Figure 2.16   Erasing a File

```
A>erase format.com

A>dir format.com

 Volume in drive A has no label
 Directory of  A:\

File not found

A>_
```

Step 2: Erasing Several Files All at Once

By using the global file name characters * and ?, you can tell DOS to erase several files with a single ERASE command. In fact, you can even wipe out every file on the whole disk. Although this is often useful to clear off a disk, it should be used with care. Make sure that your DOS Startup disk copy is in drive A, and enter this command:

   erase *.*

Because this is a potentially disastrous command if entered by mistake, DOS will ask you if you're sure you want to do this. If you enter **y** for yes, DOS will go ahead and erase everything. If you say **n** for no, DOS will immediately cancel the ERASE command. You will only get this chance to back out, however, if you use the *.* designation. If you enter **erase *.exe**, DOS does not ask you if you're sure and immediately deletes all files with an extension of EXE. So again, *be careful* with the ERASE command!

   Answer **y** to erase all the files and enter **dir** to examine the disk directory. Your screen should look like Figure 2.17.

Lesson 14: Displaying a Text File

So far, you've learned quite a bit about manipulating files with DOS. You haven't, however, yet looked inside one. The DOS TYPE command lets you display the contents of a file on the screen. Although TYPE will work with almost any file, unless it's a text file all you'll see is gibberish on the screen. A text file is one that is produced by a text editor or word processing program. Unfortunately, none of the files on the DOS disks are text files; they are all program files or system files. So, for the next two lessons we're going to use an interesting application of the COPY command to create a sample text file. Then we'll show you how to display that file on your screen and print it out.

Figure 2.17   Erasing All the Files

```
A>erase *.*
Are you sure (Y/N)?y

A>dir

 Volume in drive A has no label
 Directory of  A:\

File not found

A>_
```

Step 1: Create a Sample Text File

DOS has an interesting feature that lets you treat certain devices, such as the keyboard/screen combination or the printer, as if they were files. These devices are given reserved names that you can use as if they were file names. For example, the keyboard and screen together are given the reserved name CON, which stands for console. Similarly, the primary printer connected to the computer can be referred to as PRN. You can use these *device names* in DOS commands as if they were file names.

We're going to use this feature along with the COPY command to create a text file. Put the new diskette you first formatted in Lesson 8 into disk drive A and enter this command:

copy con readme.txt

This command tells DOS to take everything you now type at the keyboard and copy it into a new file named README.TXT. Type the following text, pressing the **Enter** key at the end of each line:

> This is a sample text file created to demonstrate the
> use of the DOS TYPE and PRINT commands. A text file is
> simply a file that contains only letters, numbers,
> punctuation marks, and other symbols that appear on the
> keyboard. Normally, text files are created with a text
> editor or word processing program. You can, however,
> create small text files directly from DOS by using the
> COPY command with the device name CON. When you are
> finished entering text, you must press the F6 function
> key and then the Enter key to generate an end-of-file
> code and have DOS copy the text file to your disk.

As the paragraph says, when you are finished entering the last line, press the **F6** function key and then press the **Enter** key. This inserts the DOS end-of-file code and completes the COPY command. Now enter **dir** to confirm that you have created the file on your disk. At this point, your screen should look like Figure 2.18.

Figure 2.18   Creating a Text File

```
A>copy con readme.txt
This is a sample text file created to demonstrate the
use of the DOS TYPE and PRINT commands.  A text file is
simply a file that contains only letters, numbers,
punctuation marks, and other symbols that appear on the
keyboard.  Normally, text files are created with a text
editor or word processing program.  You can, however,
create small text files directly from DOS by using the
COPY command with the device name CON.  When you are
finished entering text, you must press the F6 function
key and then the Enter key to generate an end-of-file
code and have DOS copy the text file to your disk.
^Z
        1 File(s) copied

A>dir

 Volume in drive A has no label
 Directory of  A:\

README   TXT      595   7-14-88  11:54a
        1 File(s)     308224 bytes free

A>_
```

Step 2: Issue the TYPE Command

There's now a file named README.TXT on your disk in drive A. You can see the contents of this file by using the DOS TYPE command. To use the TYPE command, simply enter **type** followed by the name of the file you wish to display. Enter this command to see what's in the file README.TXT:

    type readme.txt

DOS will then display the contents of README.TXT on your screen, as shown in Figure 2.19.

Figure 2.19   Displaying a Text File

```
A>type readme.txt
This is a sample text file created to demonstrate the
use of the DOS TYPE and PRINT commands.  A text file is
simply a file that contains only letters, numbers,
punctuation marks, and other symbols that appear on the
keyboard.  Normally, text files are created with a text
editor or word processing program.  You can, however,
create small text files directly from DOS by using the
COPY command with the device name CON.  When you are
finished entering text, you must press the F6 function
key and then the Enter key to generate an end-of-file
code and have DOS copy the text file to your disk.

A>_
```

Lesson 15: Printing a Text File

Most text files eventually wind up on paper; after all, the end product of word processing is usually a hard copy document. The DOS PRINT command lets you send a text file directly to the printer, instead of displaying it on the screen. You'll need a printer for this lesson, as well as the diskette with the README.TXT file you created in Lesson 14.

Step 1: Put the DOS Operating Disk in Drive A

Unlike TYPE, the PRINT command is an external command that resides on the DOS Operating diskette. (DOS versions prior to 3.30 have the PRINT command on the diskette labeled DOS.) So, you must first put the disk containing the PRINT command into drive A. If your computer has two floppy drives, put the disk containing README.TXT in drive B.

Step 2: Turn on Your Printer

Before you can print a file, your printer must be turned on. Make sure that the power is on and that the printer is on-line, that is, connected to your computer.

Step 3: Issue the PRINT Command

To use the PRINT command, just type PRINT followed by the name of the file you want to print. You can preface the name of the file by the letter of the disk drive on which it is stored. Even if your computer has only one floppy drive, enter this command:

print b:readme.txt

After you do this, DOS will ask you to supply the following:

```
Name of list device [PRN]:
```

This rather cryptic request allows you to tell DOS which printer to use if you have more than one connected to your computer. The expression [PRN] means that unless you tell it otherwise, DOS will send the output to the default printer, which has the device name PRN. If you have only one printer, then it is the default printer. All you have to do here is just press the **Enter** key. DOS will ask you to supply the list device only the first time you use PRINT for any given computer session.

If you have a B floppy drive in your computer, PRINT will inform you that it's currently printing README.TXT and your printer should be merrily pounding away (unless, of course, it's a laser or ink-jet printer). Figure 2.20 shows what you should see on your screen.

If your computer only has one floppy drive, then DOS will ask you to do the following:

```
Insert diskette for drive B: and strike any key when ready.
```

Figure 2.20   Printing a Text File

```
A>print b:readme.txt
Name of list device [PRN]:
Resident part of PRINT installed

    B:\README.TXT is currently being printed

A>_
```

This is an example of a handy DOS feature. If you have only an A drive, and you issue a command that refers to drive B, DOS will temporarily pretend that drive A is drive B. It will then ask you to insert into drive A the disk you would have put into drive B if you had a drive B. So, if you have only one floppy drive, put the README.TXT disk in drive A when you get this message and press any key to finish the printing process.

The end result of this PRINT command will be a printout of the text in file README.TXT that you saw on your screen when you used the TYPE command in Lesson 14.

Lesson 16: Running a Program

This lesson won't really teach you anything new, because you've been running programs throughout this entire chapter. Every time you entered a DOS command, you were running a program. Remember: files with an EXE or COM extension are executable programs that you can run.

Step 1: Insert the Appropriate Disk

Just as you have to put the appropriate DOS disk in drive A when you want to use an external command, you must make sure a program is stored on a disk in one of your drives when you want to run the program. For example, to run an application program such as dBASE III PLUS, you must have its disk in the A or B drive. Or, if your computer has a hard disk, you could run the program off the C drive provided that a copy resides there. If your computer is connected to a local area network, you could run the program if it's stored on your network's server disk. DOS must be able to find a program before it can be run.

Step 2: Switch to the Appropriate Drive, if Necessary

For example, if you have two floppy drives, the DOS disk in A, and the application's program disk in B, you could switch to drive B as you learned in Lesson 5. The alternative to switching drives is to preface the program name you enter with the letter of the drive on which the program's file is stored.

Step 3: Type the Program Name and Press the Enter Key

As you now know, you invoke an external DOS command by entering its name along with any necessary file names and other information. In this sense, application programs such as dBASE III PLUS are the same as DOS external commands; all you have to do to run them is type the name of the EXE or COM file in which they're stored and press the **Enter** key. So, for example, to run the dBASE III PLUS program off your current default drive, just type **dbase** and press the **Enter** key. Or, if your default drive is A and the dBASE III PLUS disk is in drive B, you could enter **b:dbase** from the A drive to run the program. When you do either of these, DOS will load the dBASE III PLUS program into primary memory and begin executing it.

Lesson 17: Working with Subdirectories

As you can imagine, people who use microcomputers extensively often generate large numbers of files. Before hard disks became common, users had many different floppy disks on which to store their files. Organizing files meant physically organizing diskettes by keeping them well-labeled and storing them in subdivided boxes, racks, or cabinets. Once hard disks became common, however, operating systems had to devise a better method of organizing large numbers of files. Even a modest 20-megabyte hard disk can store thousands of different files. Looking for a particular file among hundreds or thousands of files is time consuming and tedious. Consequently, most microcomputer operating systems, including DOS, have evolved a **hierarchical** method of organizing files into groups. Such a system allows you to cluster files into orders or ranks, each subordinate to the one above. These groups of files, called **subdirectories**, are like file folders that can be nested within one another. Disks can be organized into subdirectories, each of which can contain files and other subdirectories.

Subdirectories are invaluable tools for organizing programs and data files on high-capacity storage devices. In addition, subdirectories make it easier for the operating system to locate a particular file because large numbers of files are divided into smaller groups. Although subdirectories are most often, indeed almost always, found on hard disks, they are occasionally used on floppy disks, too. DOS includes commands that let you create, access, and remove subdirectories.

With DOS, every disk has a single main directory, known as the **root directory**. DOS automatically creates a root directory on every disk you format. This is the directory you are in when you first boot up DOS or when you first change your default drive. The root directory itself has no name, but it's represented by a backslash (\).

Step 1: Create a Subdirectory

Let's create a subdirectory on the new floppy disk you have used in previous lessons (the one with README.TXT on it). Put this disk into drive A, and enter this command:

md a:\text

The internal DOS command MD or MKDIR (short for Make Directory) is used to create a new subdirectory. It is followed by **the path** of the new subdirectory. The path is an optional disk drive specifier followed by a list of subdirectory names, separated by backslashes. The rules for naming subdirectories are the same as the rules for naming files. The simplest path is a single backslash \, which represents the root directory of your current default drive. The command you just entered creates a subdirectory named TEXT on the disk in drive A. This subdirectory is one level below the root directory.

Step 2: Change to the Subdirectory

Think of the subdirectory as a separate "sub-disk" on your disk. Enter **dir** to display a directory of your disk. Now enter the Change Directory (CD or CHDIR) command to move into your new subdirectory:

cd a:\text

Enter **dir** again and Figure 2.21 shows what you should see on your screen. The first DIR gives a directory listing of the root directory of the floppy disk. It contains the README.TXT file and the TEXT subdirectory. The second DIR gives a directory listing inside the TEXT subdirectory.

Figure 2.21   Changing to a Subdirectory

```
A>md a:\text

A>dir

 Volume in drive A has no label
 Directory of  A:\

README   TXT      595   7-14-88  11:54a
TEXT          <DIR>      7-14-88   2:31p
        2 File(s)    307200 bytes free

A>cd a:\text

A>dir

 Volume in drive A has no label
 Directory of  A:\TEXT

.             <DIR>      7-14-88   2:31p
..            <DIR>      7-14-88   2:31p
        2 File(s)    307200 bytes free

A>_
```

Step 3: Copy a File to the Subdirectory

Right now, the TEXT subdirectory has no ordinary user files in it. You can, how-ever, copy your own files to this subdirectory just as if it were a separate disk. For example, let's copy the README.TXT file from the root directory to the TEXT subdirectory. Enter this command:

copy a:\readme.txt

This command copies the file README.TXT from the root directory of drive A to your current subdirectory, which happens to be TEXT. Now enter **dir** and you'll see that a copy of README.TXT now also exists in the TEXT subdirectory. It's important to realize that there are two separate copies of README.TXT now on the disk: one in the root directory and one in the TEXT subdirectory.

Step 4: Remove the Subdirectory

Once you're in a subdirectory, you can almost think of it as a separate disk. You can run programs from within a subdirectory. Many DOS commands that deal with files will operate only on the files in your current subdirectory unless you specify otherwise. For example, you can delete every file in a subdirectory without affecting any files in the root directory or any other subdirectories. For example, try entering this command:

erase *.*

Answer **y** for yes when the ERASE command asks if you are sure that this is what you want to do. DOS will erase every file in your current directory, the TEXT sub-directory. Enter **dir** to see that this is true. Now change back to the root directory by entering this command:

cd a:

Now enter another DIR command and you will see that the README.TXT file in the root is still intact.

Just as you must occasionally delete unneeded files, sometimes subdirectories must be removed, too. Let's say that you are finished with the TEXT subdirectory and you want to remove it from your disk. To do this you must first erase any files inside the subdirectory and move out of the subdirectory. We've already done this. Now you can enter the Remove Directory command (RD or RMDIR) to remove the empty TEXT subdirectory from your disk:

rd a:\text

If you enter **dir**, you will see that the TEXT subdirectory has indeed been removed, and your disk is the same as it was when you began this lesson.

Lesson 18: Using Batch Files

A **batch file** is a text file that contains a list of commands or programs to be run. Batch files are usually created with a text editor or word processing program, but you can easily create short ones using the COPY command method we outlined in Step 1 of Lesson 14. In DOS, every batch file must have an extension of BAT. Once it has been created, a batch file is invoked by typing its filename and pressing the **Enter** key. When this is done, DOS executes each command or program listed in the batch file, one at a time. DOS includes features that enable experienced users to construct complex and very helpful batch files. Even if you never actually make your own batch files, you will undoubtedly use some made by others or included with application packages. As an example, let's create and use a simple batch file.

Step 1: Create the Batch File

As we said, batch files are usually created with a text editor or word processor. Short ones, however, can be easily created with the COPY command. At this point, you should still have the floppy disk with the README.TXT file on it in drive A. Enter this command to create a new batch file named SHOW.BAT on your current disk:

copy con show.bat

Now you can enter the text that will go inside the file SHOW.BAT. Type the following three commands, pressing the **Enter** key after each one:

cls
dir
type readme.txt

Finally, press the **F6** function key to generate the end-of-file code and then press the **Enter** key. Enter **dir** to examine the current contents of your disk and see that the batch file has indeed been created. Your screen should look like Figure 2.22.

Figure 2.22   Creating a Batch File

```
A>copy con show.bat
cls
dir
type readme.txt
^Z
         1 File(s) copied

A>dir

 Volume in drive A has no label
 Directory of  A:\

README   TXT     595   7-14-88  11:54a
SHOW     BAT      27   7-15-88   9:14a
         2 File(s)    387200 bytes free

A>_
```

Step 2: Use the Batch File

Running a batch file is just like executing a command or running an application program. You type its filename (without the extension) and press the Enter key. To run your newly created batch file, simply type **show** and press the **Enter** key. Figure 2.23 shows the result.

Figure 2.23   Using a Batch File

```
A>dir

 Volume in drive A has no label
 Directory of  A:\

README    TXT      595    7-14-88   11:54a
SHOW      BAT       27    7-15-88    9:14a
         2 File(s)    307200 bytes free

A>type readme.txt
This is a sample text file created to demonstrate the
use of the DOS TYPE and PRINT commands.  A text file is
simply a file that contains only letters, numbers,
punctuation marks, and other symbols that appear on the
keyboard.  Normally, text files are created with a text
editor or word processing program.  You can, however,
create small text files directly from DOS by using the
COPY command with the device name CON.  When you are
finished entering text, you must press the F6 function
key and then the Enter key to generate an end-of-file
code and have DOS copy the text file to your disk.

A>
A>_
```

Most commands and programs that you can run directly from the DOS prompt can be put inside a batch file. Batch files allow you to automate frequently executed series of commands. They also allow experts to set up complex sequences of commands to be run by novices. For example, many new application programs must be installed on your system before you can use them. In some cases, this installation process can be quite involved. Most software developers, therefore, include one or more batch files that make the installation process much easier for users.

The AUTOEXEC.BAT File The most commonly used batch file is a special one named AUTOEXEC.BAT–the auto-execute batch file. Whenever you boot up your computer, DOS searches the root directory of the current drive for this AUTOEXEC.BAT file. If there is no AUTOEXEC.BAT file present, DOS simply asks you to supply the current date and time, and then presents its prompt. If, on the other hand, AUTOEXEC.BAT is found, then that batch file is automatically executed. Since the AUTOEXEC.BAT file is automatically invoked every time you boot up your computer, it is ideal for listing any commands and programs you always run when you first turn on your machine. For example, if there is a subdirectory that you always use, you could put a CD (Change Directory) command in the AUTOEXEC.BAT to move into that subdirectory. Most DOS users eventually set up their own AUTOEXEC.BAT files or have someone else help them do so.

Conclusion

In this chapter of the *Software Guide*, you've learned several of the most frequently used DOS commands. To be sure, we haven't covered every DOS command or discussed every feature of this rich and powerful operating system. Most computer users, however, find that they primarily spend their time running application programs such as dBASE III PLUS. Their direct interaction with DOS is, for the most part, on the level of the commands and procedures we've introduced in this chapter. To learn even more about DOS, consult one of the many books completely devoted to the subject. Or, refer to the documentation provided by IBM and Microsoft: the *DOS User's Guide* and the *DOS Reference* manual.

Exercises

Multiple Choice

Choose the best selection to complete each statement.

_____ 1. An operating system is a(n)
   a. hardware component of a mainframe computer system.
   b. application program that produces text files.
   c. set of programs that lets you use your computer's hardware and software resources.
   d. system of procedures for operating a computer.

_____ 2. Transient routines or external commands are
   (a) kept in primary memory until the computer is shut off.
   (b) kept on disk and loaded into memory only when needed.
   (c) kept in ROM (read-only memory) chips.
   (d) used once then deleted.

_____ 3. The driving force behind each new DOS release has usually been
   (a) the addition of a new disk drive capability.
   (b) an effort to improve the user interface.
   (c) an attempt to eliminate all bugs.
   (d) an effort by IBM and Microsoft to make more money.

_____ 4. Upwardly compatible means that
   (a) you cannot take advantage of the new version's abilities.
   (b) all old software versions must be upgraded.
   (c) new hardware must be purchased to use the new version.
   (d) operations that worked with former versions work with the new version.

_____ 5. A command is a(n)
   (a) combination of hardware switch settings.
   (b) operating system directive issued to a user.
   (c) application package instruction.
   (d) word or abbreviation that tells DOS to run a program.

_____ 6. To boot DOS with the power off
   (a) insert the DOS disk and turn on the power.
   (b) hold down the Control, Alternate, and Delete keys at the same time.
   (c) turn the power on and issue the boot command.
   (d) turn the power on and kick the computer.

_____ 7. Pressing Ctrl-Alt-Del will
   (a) invoke a DOS transient routine.
   (b) delete a file.
   (c) reboot DOS without having to shut off the computer.
   (d) execute an application program.

_____ 8. The DOS directory command is
   (a) DIRECT.
   (b) LIST.
   (c) DIR.
   (d) CATALOG.

_____ 9. The two parts of a DOS file name are
   (a) a disk drive designation and a disk sector number.
   (b) a primary file name and an optional extension.
   (c) a primary file name and a creation date.
   (d) a primary extension and the size in bytes.

_____ 10. Files with COM and EXE extensions usually designate
   (a) external commands and   (c) configuration files and batch files.
       executable program files.   (d) BASIC and FORTRAN files.
   (b) command files and extension files.

_____ 11. Pressing Ctrl-Num Lock or Pause will
   (a) echo input and output to the   (c) cancel a command.
       printer.   (d) temporarily halt screen scrolling.
   (b) print the screen.

_____ 12. To change the default disk drive
   (a) put a new disk in drive A.   (c) open up the computer and replace
   (b) type the new disk drive   the faulty drive.
       designation and press Enter.   (d) issue the DIR command.

_____ 13. To display a disk and memory status report, enter
   (a) status.   (c) chkdsk.
   (b) dir.   (d) diskcopy.

_____ 14. Formatting a diskette does not
   (a) check the diskette for bad sectors. (c) mark off the space into sectors.
   (b) wipe out all data on the diskette. (d) sort files in the directory.

_____ 15. To format a system diskette you must
   (a) reboot the system.   (c) enter the COPY command.
   (b) use the /s parameter with the   (d) purchase a master diskette from
       FORMAT command.   IBM.

_____ 16. One way to copy every file from disk drive A to B is to
   (a) enter copy a:*.* b:.   (c) enter copy a: b:.
   (b) enter dir a: b:.   (d) use the REN command.

_____ 17. To make an exact copy of an entire diskette, use
   (a) COPY.   (c) DIR.
   (b) DISKCOPY.   (d) Ctrl-Alt-Del.

_____ 18. Entering the command del *.* will
   (a) reboot the system.   (c) rename all files on the disk in the
   (b) copy all files to the disk in the   default drive.
       default drive.   (d) erase all files from the disk in the
                                            default drive.

_____ 19. To display a text file on your screen use the
   (a) PRINT command.   (c) TYPE command.
   (b) DISKCOPY command.   (d) Ctrl-Num Lock key.

_____ 20. To run a program or batch file you must
   (a) type its filename and press the (c) press Ctrl-Break.
       Enter key.   (d) first make a backup copy.
   (b) reboot DOS.

Fill-In

1. A disk operating system has many utilities for dealing with the _____ that are stored on disks.

2. _____ is usually used with IBM computers while _____ is usually used with compatible computers such as those made by Compaq, AT&T, Tandy, and Zenith.

3. Booting DOS refers to the process of loading the disk operating system into _____.

4. In many cases, when you first boot DOS it asks you to enter the _____ and the _____.

5. The _____ command can be used to list the names, sizes, and creation dates and times of all the files on a disk.

6. A file's primary filename can have from one to _____ characters in it.

7. File name extensions are often used to _____ files.

8. You can press the _____ key to cancel a command if you haven't pressed the Enter key yet.

9. You can press _____ to cancel a command before it finishes normally.

10. The DOS _____ indicates the current default disk drive.

11. The _____ command can tell you how much memory is installed in your computer.

12. A diskette must be _____ before it can be used to store program and data files.

13. The _____ command can be used to duplicate one or more files on the same or on different disks.

14. _____ file name characters can be used to refer to several files at the same time.

15. The DISKCOPY command will automatically _____ the target diskette if it's brand new.

16. The REN command can be used to _____ one or more file names.

17. To remove a file from a disk, you would enter _____ or _____ followed by the file's name.

18. The TYPE command lets you display _____ files on your screen.

19. You could use the _____ command to produce a hard copy of a text file.

20. The DOS commands used to create, change to, and remove subdirectories are _____, _____, and _____.

Short Problems

1. If you have access to a diskette other than the DOS floppies, produce a directory listing of the files on it. If you have a printer, try using Ctrl-PrtSc to turn on printer echoing before you issue the directory command so that you can get a hard copy.

2. When you booted DOS, you were asked to supply the date and time. Two DOS commands, DATE and TIME, tell you the current date and time and let you change these settings. Try the DATE and TIME commands. If you don't want to change the date and time settings, just press the Enter key when asked for the new date or time. Notice how DOS automatically figures out and displays the day of the week.

3. Use the * global file name character to produce a directory listing of all the files on the DOS Startup disk with an EXE extension.

4. Use the * global file name character to produce a directory listing of all the files on the DOS Startup disk whose names begin with the letter K.

5. Use the ? global file name character to produce a directory listing of all the files on the DOS Startup disk that have an E as the second letter of their primary filenames.

6. You've probably noticed the "Volume in drive A has no label" message DOS gives when it displays a directory of the DOS disk. The FORMAT command has an option that lets you specify a name for a disk, or volume label as DOS calls it. Try formatting a blank disk with this command:

   format b:/v

   If you have only one floppy drive, enter this instead:

   format a:/v

   The /V is an optional parameter that tells the FORMAT command to ask you for a volume label. Think up a name of 11 characters or less and enter it when FORMAT tells you to. When you're done, check the disk's directory to see your volume label displayed.

7. DOS versions 3.0 and newer have a command that lets you supply or change a volume label without having to reformat a disk. If you have DOS 3.0 or newer try using the LABEL command on the new disk you've just formatted. Note that you can't change the label of the original DOS disk because it's write-protected.

8. If you don't know what DOS version you have, enter **ver**. This command displays the number of the DOS version you are using.

9. Another way to find out the volume label of a disk is to use the VOL command. Enter **vol a:**. This command displays the volume label (if there is one) of the disk in drive A.

10. It is possible to display a text file on your screen by using the COPY command instead of the TYPE command. In certain cases, DOS can refer to its peripheral devices as if they were files. There are several file names that have a special meaning to DOS. These are called DOS device names. For example, CON refers to the console, or the keyboard and screen. Put the disk with your README.TXT file in drive A and enter this command:

    copy readme.txt con

    You should see the text of file README.TXT displayed on your screen just as if you used the TYPE command.

11. Just as CON is a DOS device name that refers to the keyboard and screen, PRN is a DOS device name that refers to the printer. Try using the COPY command to get a printout of the README.TXT file.

12. The DIR command has two optional parameters that can be useful when looking at disks with lots of files on them. The /P parameter will automatically pause the display when the screen is full and let you press a key to continue. The /W parameter will display the directory in a wide format across the screen, omitting the sizes and creation dates and times so that more file names will fit at once. Put your DOS Startup disk in drive A and try entering these options:

    dir /p
    dir /w

3

dBASE III PLUS

By the end of this chapter, you should be able to do the following:

- Invoke the dBASE III PLUS program
- Use the dBASE III PLUS Assistant menu system
- Create a data base structure
- Input data base records
- List, browse, retrieve, and display data base records
- Append new records to an existing data base
- Modify existing data base records

- Delete data base records
- Search a data base for one or more records
- Update and delete records throughout an entire data base
- Modify the structure of an existing data base
- Create a report layout and generate a data base report
- Sort a data base
- Index a data base

Introduction

One of the most common tasks entrusted to computers is managing the information kept on secondary storage media like floppy and hard disks. Since virtually all of this information is organized into files, programs that enable users to manipulate files are extremely valuable. Anyone who handles files can benefit from a system that enables the user to create, add to, delete from, update, sort, rearrange, select from, print out, and otherwise manage files. dBASE III PLUS is a sophisticated information storage and retrieval system designed for IBM and IBM-compatible microcomputers.

As you may already know, a file is a collection of data organized into records. A record is a collection of fields, each of which in turn is a collection of adjacent characters. One or more files of efficiently stored, interrelated data items is commonly known as a data base (or database, as it's also written). In this sense dBASE III PLUS is a powerful, general-purpose data base management system that uses the relational model of data base design. A relational data base organizes data elements into two-dimensional tables of rows and columns. The rows represent data records and the columns are fields within those records. An advanced feature of a relational data base manager like dBASE III PLUS is that it can draw information from several different files linked by a common field. Such software packages are ideal for managing mailing lists, inventories, customer accounts, price lists, telephone directories, bibliographies, and many other kinds of data bases.

Specifically speaking, dBASE III PLUS is an improved version of dBASE III, which itself is a successor to dBASE II. dBASE II, the first widely popular data base manager for microcomputers, was originally called Vulcan (after the home planet of "Star Trek's" Mr. Spock) by its original creator. Wayne Ratliff developed Vulcan while working as a software systems designer for NASA's Jet Propulsion Laboratory. He turned over the marketing of Vulcan to a newly formed software distributing company called Ashton-Tate. In January 1981, Ashton-Tate renamed the product dBASE II. By 1983, dBASE II had sold over 200,000 copies.

Responding to technical advances in microcomputer hardware and software, Ashton-Tate released dBASE III in May 1984. dBASE III was specially designed to take advantage of the power of 16-bit computers like the IBM PC. It was faster and more efficient than dBASE II and had a much greater storage capacity. Introduced in late 1985, dBASE III PLUS was intended to meet the needs of customers who wanted an even more powerful, user-friendly package that would also work on local area networks. dBASE III PLUS does provide greater processing speed than dBASE III and adds networking capabilities. But more important from the standpoint of the average u8ser is its new interactive menu system. Novice users can perform most common operations by selecting options from menus rather than by typing commands that must be memorized or looked up in the manual. As they become more skilled, users can gradually learn the commands that will give them access to more powerful capabilities. For the lessons of this chapter, we'll be using dBASE III PLUS version 1.1.

General Features of dBASE III PLUS

Virtually everyone in the industry agrees that Ashton-Tate's dBASE family is the market leader in microcomputer data base management. dBASE has a long history and a very widespread following of devoted users. Although it's an extremely sophisticated package with many capabilities beyond the novice user, dBASE III PLUS offers a comprehensive set of basic features that are easy for beginners to learn and use. We'll concentrate on these most commonly used features. Some of the things you can do with dBASE III PLUS include:

- **Using Menus** dBASE III PLUS has a sophisticated menu system that's especially easy for beginners to use. It presents boxes containing clearly labeled options. All you do is highlight the item you want and press a key to make your choice.

- **Getting Help** Available at the press of a single key is an extensive help facility that can provide information about the command with which you're currently working.

- **Creating Data Base Structures** You can easily create a new data base by specifying precisely how your information is to be arranged in storage. All you have to do is specify the name, type, and length of each data item in a record.

- **Entering Data Base Records** dBASE III PLUS enables you to add records to a data base with little effort. It displays a blank data entry form on your screen with all the fields labeled. Data items are simply keyed into empty fields.

- **Examining Existing Data Bases** Several ways to retrieve and display data base records are provided. You can specify a single record, select a group of records, or browse through an entire data base. Output can be displayed on the screen or directed to a printer.

- **Modifying Existing Records** Changing the contents of an existing data base record is as easy as displaying them. Corrections and updates can be made to one or several records.

- **Deleting Records** It's a simple matter to purge information that's no longer needed with dBASE III PLUS. Furthermore, there's a built-in safety feature that gives you a chance to change your mind and recall a deleted record.

- **Finding Existing Records** You can search a data base for one particular record. In addition, you can also locate and retrieve groups of records that share common attributes.

- **Updating throughout a Whole Data Base** With a single command, dBASE III PLUS gives you the ability to update one or more fields in an entire data base. You can even search through all the records and delete selected ones.

- **Modifying Existing Data Base Structures** You can add items to data records, change their names, and even change certain storage characteristics without having to reenter all your data.

- **Generating Data Base Reports** dBASE III PLUS lets you define and save the layout of a data base report. Reports can be merely displayed on the screen or also sent to a printer.

- **Sorting Data Base Records** You can rearrange the contents of a data base according to the information stored in one or any number of fields, creating a new data base file in the process.

- **Indexing Data Base Records** In addition to sorting, dBASE III PLUS also lets you create index files that control the order in which data base records are displayed and printed.

Getting Started

As we've mentioned before, dBASE III PLUS is quite a sophisticated software package. When purchased from Ashton-Tate, it comes with two thick documentation manuals and eight floppy disks. The basic dBASE III PLUS program, however, is stored on just two diskettes, labeled System Disk #1 and System Disk #2. You're most likely to use dBASE III PLUS in one of three possible arrangements:

1. On a microcomputer with two floppy drives with dBASE III PLUS on System Disks 1 and 2.
2. On a microcomputer with a hard disk and a floppy drive with dBASE III PLUS installed on the hard disk.
3. On a microcomputer connected to a local area network with dBASE III PLUS installed on the network's disk server.

All of these arrangements require configuring DOS so that it can handle dBASE's use of files. Hard disks and networks also require a special installation procedure. Although these setup procedures aren't difficult, they should already be done for you at your particular computer installation. You may need some simple directions from your instructor on how to access dBASE III PLUS, but once you're situated, you should be able to do the following lessons as they're described.

Lesson 1: Running dBASE III PLUS

Assuming that dBASE III PLUS has been installed and your computer system is properly configured, you are ready to work with data bases. The first thing to do is call up and execute the dBASE III PLUS program.

Step 1: Boot up DOS

If your computer has two floppy drives, put your DOS disk in drive A, close the door, and turn on the system unit. If your computer has a hard disk or is connected to a local area network, just turn it on. If your display is a color monitor (with three knobs on the front), turn it on by twisting the top knob. Finally, if a printer is attached, turn that on too. Enter the date and time to complete the DOS boot-up process as we described in Lesson 1 of Chapter 1.

Step 2: Insert dBASE III PLUS System Disk #1 or Switch to the dBASE Subdirectory

For two-floppy systems, remove your DOS disk from drive A and replace it with your dBASE III PLUS System Disk #1. If you're using a computer with a hard disk or one that is connected to a local area network, this step is unnecessary. In these cases, however, you may have to follow some simple directions from your instructor to enable you to access dBASE III PLUS on your particular system. For example, on a hard disk system, you may have to switch to the dBASE subdirectory by entering **cd c:\dbase**.

Step 3: Invoke dBASE III PLUS

Once you get situated in the proper disk drive directory, running dBASE III PLUS is easy. All you have to do is type **dbase** and press **Enter**. It will take a minute or so for dBASE III PLUS to be loaded from the disk into your computer's primary memory. If you're working on a computer with a hard disk (like we're using to produce these figures), then your screen will clear and Figure 3.1 will pop up.

Figure 3.1   dBASE III PLUS Identification Screen, License Agreement, and Command Line

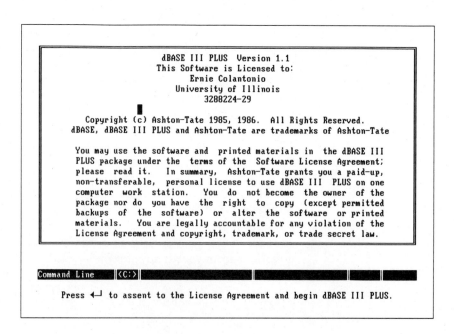

This screen identifies the dBASE III PLUS version and presents Ashton-Tate's License Agreement. The bright bar across the bottom is called the command line, about which we'll have more to say later in this chapter. At the very bottom is the message line, which is used to give you instructions, hints, and other pertinent information. Follow the directions and press **Enter** to begin dBASE III PLUS.

If you're working on a computer with two floppy drives instead of a hard disk or network, the message line will be:

```
Insert System Disk 2 and press ENTER, or press Ctrl-C to abort.
```

You're being prompted to remove System Disk #1 from drive A, replace it with System Disk #2, and press **Enter**. This extra step is necessary with two-floppy systems because the entire dBASE III PLUS program won't fit on a single diskette. Once the rest of the program is loaded, you'll also be prompted to press **Enter** to begin dBASE III PLUS.

Lesson 2: Using the dBASE III PLUS Assistant

The original dBASE II program is strictly a command-driven system. In other words, you tell it what to do by entering commands at a prompt just like you do with DOS. This system is fast and powerful, but it requires that you memorize commands or constantly look them up in the manual if you don't remember them. dBASE III provided as an option a simple menu system called ASSIST. For dBASE III PLUS, Ashton-Tate expanded and improved this menu system into what's now known as The Assistant. Although you can still use commands, just like with dBASE II and dBASE III, most beginners use The Assistant interactive menu system to tell dBASE III PLUS what to do.

Step 1: Examine the Current Menu Screen

Whether you start dBASE III PLUS from floppy, hard disk, or network, the Opening menu you see on your screen will look almost the same. The default disk drive may be specified differently, but your screen should now look like Figure 3.2.

Figure 3.2   dBASE III PLUS Opening Menu

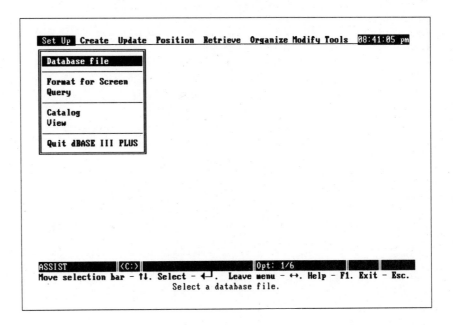

The very top line is called the menu bar; it contains the main Assistant menu options and the current time of day at the far right. The reverse video highlight block shows that the Set Up option is currently selected. Below is a box that contains a submenu of options that relate to the Set Up option. It too has a highlight block that shows the submenu option (Database file) that is currently selected. Depending on the currently selected option, the number of submenu options may vary. In addition, some menu options cause yet other submenus to pop up. The long bright bar across the bottom of the screen is called the status bar. It shows that you are using The Assistant and displays the current disk drive, the current menu option or record number, and the status of the Insert and Caps Lock keys. Above the status bar is the action line. Although it's blank now, the action line shows the dBASE III PLUS command generated by the current Assistant operation. Below the status bar is the navigation line, which tells you how to move about between menu or submenu options. Finally, below the navigation line at the very bottom of the screen is the message line. It describes the current operation and the entry you are supposed to make.

Step 2: Explore the Other Menu Options

Press the **Down** and **Up Arrow** keys to move the submenu highlight block. Position it on the option you want and press **Enter** to select it. To move between the major options in the menu bar, use the **Left** and **Right Arrow** keys. Notice how new submenus pop up as you move the highlight block. Another way to move within the menu bar is to press the key of the first letter of the option. For example, press **T** to move to the Tools option.

If you make a mistake and select an option you really don't want, you can cancel that operation by pressing **Escape**. Each time you press Escape, dBASE III PLUS will go back one level to the previous submenu choice. If you press Escape while you're at the Main menu, you'll exit The Assistant and enter the command mode. dBASE III PLUS will present you with its command prompt, which consists of a single period, or dot as it's also called. To get back to The Assistant, simply enter **assist** at the dot prompt.

Step 3: Explore the Help Facility

Every time you select an item from the Assistant menu, dBASE III PLUS translates that selection into the corresponding command. This command is what you see on the action line when you execute an option. One way to find out more about a particular option or command is to look it up in the dBASE manual. Another way is to use the dBASE III PLUS help facility. All you have to do is press the F1 key. dBASE III PLUS will display a screen of information about the command that corresponds to the currently selected menu item. For example, use the **Right** or **Left Arrow** key to move the highlight bar to the Set Up option. Now use the **Up** or **Down Arrow** key to move the submenu highlight bar to the Quit dBASE III option. Press **F1** and you'll see Figue 3.3.

When you're done reading the help message, press **Enter** to return to the Assistant menu. Move around the various Assistant options and explore the help facility further. Obviously, you can learn quite a bit about dBASE III PLUS with just the F1 key.

Figure 3.3   The Quit Option

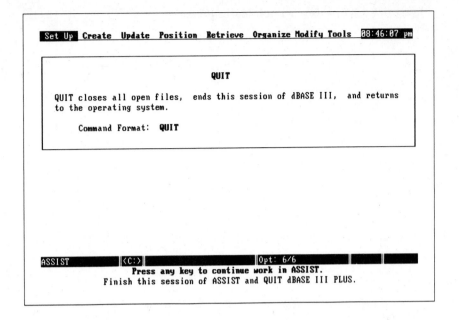

Lesson 3: Defining the Data Base Structure

As we've been doing throughout this manual, we're going to introduce an example and suggest that you follow along at you own computer. The example that we'll use is the customer mailing list of a fictional locksmith business. Figure 3.4 shows the Kwik Key & Lock mailing list.

This file is a date base; the rows are records; and the columns are fields. In order to be managed and manipulated by dBASE, the data must first be entered. Before that, however, you have to tell dBASE how to structure the data base.

Step 1: Select the Create Option

Use the **Left** or **Right Arrow** key to move the highlight block to the Create option in the menu bar at the top of the screen. When you select the Create option, the first submenu option under it, Database file, is automatically highlighted (see Figure 3.5). Notice also that close to the middle of the status bar along the bottom the program says Opt: 1/6. This message, along with the submenu highlight block, indicates that the first option out of six possible options is the one that is currently selected. Press **Enter** to invoke this option and create a new data base. You should see the following message appear in the action line above the left side of the status bar along the bottom:

    Command: CREATE

Figure 3.4   Kwik Key & Lock Mailing List

Last Name	First Name	Street Address	City	State	Zip
Abel	Larry	906 Busey #5	Urbana	IL	61801
Alexander	Barbara	604 Armory	Champaign	IL	61820
Banks	David	1104 Grand Pl.	Champaign	IL	61820
Becker	Molly	310 W Paddock	Savoy	IL	61821
Calhoon	Carrie	1007 Barclay	Tolono	IL	61880
Carver	George	402 Main	Watseka	IL	60970
Crawford	John	2012 Anderson	Urbana	IL	61801
Daily	Irene	2209 Philo	Urbana	IL	61801
Davis	Becky	2504 S Lynn	Urbana	IL	61801
Diamond	Jim	502 E Chalmers	Champaign	IL	61820
Eaton	Candy	701 Dover Pl.	Champaign	IL	61820
Edwards	Barbara	1721 Valley Rd	Paxton	IL	60957
Feldman	Francis	809 W Elm	Urbana	IL	61801
Franklin	Melissa	566 W Church	Champaign	IL	61820
Garret	Gerald	1871 Parkdale	Rantoul	IL	61866
Griffith	Oscar	805 W Florida	Urbana	IL	61801
Hall	Robert	102 White	Pekin	IL	61554
Hudson	Henry	892 Bay Ave	Champaign	IL	61820
Irving	Judith	1904 Oliver Dr	Urbana	IL	61801
Jackson	Delbert	1010 W Bridle	Monticello	IL	61856
Jenkins	Alfred	311 Southmoor	Champaign	IL	61820
Jordon	Holly	1311 Grandview	Danville	IL	61832
Kelley	Joyce	142 Hazelwood	Tolono	IL	61880
Knowles	Lesley	1609 W Bradley	Champaign	IL	61820
Lancaster	Terry	805 S Randolf	Champaign	IL	61820
Lee	Kim	135 Cedar	Rantoul	IL	61866
Lowrey	Marcy	407 W Coler	Urbana	IL	61801
Malony	Fred	408 E Main	Tolono	IL	61880
McFall	Ellen	700 W Elm	Rantoul	IL	61866
Mitchell	Dan	909 Crestwood	Urbana	IL	61801
Nelson	Scott	411 E Green	Champaign	IL	61820
Novak	Sandy	3008 Kyle	Urbana	IL	61801
Olson	Roger	305 Briar Lane	Champaign	IL	61820
Owens	Diane	987 W Tremont	Monticello	IL	61856
Pearson	Charlie	605 N Willis	Tolono	IL	61880
Prorok	Brian	111 E Healy	Champaign	IL	61820
Quinlan	Kerry	809 Maple	Rantoul	IL	61866
Reeves	Mike	1507 S Race	Urbana	IL	61801
Ressel	Ruby	124 W Park	Urbana	IL	61801
Savage	Julian	114 Edgebrook	Savoy	IL	61821
Skubic	Mike	321 Gregory	Champaign	IL	61820
Spencer	Linda	506 E Oregon	Urbana	IL	61801
Townsend	Laurie	2307 Barberry	Tolono	IL	61880
Tudor	Anthony	100 Kenwood	Champaign	IL	61820
Underwood	Rhonda	1243 W Green	Urbana	IL	61801
Valentine	Paul	1325 Westwood	Monticello	IL	61856
Walden	Roxanne	134 Doddson	Urbana	IL	61801
Weaver	Sally	908 S Oak	Champaign	IL	61820
Willmann	Allison	145 E Hessel	Champaign	IL	61820
Young	Susan	508 N Edwin	Rantoul	IL	61866

Figure 3.5   The Create Option

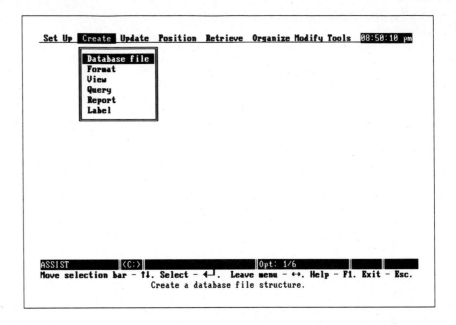

Watch this action line as you use the Assistant menu system. It indicates the dot-prompt command that corresponds to the Assistant option you've just selected. If you pay attention to the action line, it can teach you how to use dBASE III PLUS commands. As you become more skilled with dBASE III PLUS, you might discover that you prefer using dot-prompt commands to using the Assistant menus.

Step 2: Select Disk Drive

Immediately after you press Enter to create a new data base file, another submenu pops up. This submenu is a list of possible disk drive letters. If you're working off floppy drive A, the A: option will be initially highlighted. If you're using dBASE III PLUS on a hard disk, the C: option will be highlighted. To change to some other drive, you would use the Up or Down Arrow key to move the highlight block. The drive that you select is where dBASE will store your data base file. If you're using a two-floppy computer, you might want to designate drive B and insert a formatted diskette in drive B. If you're using a hard disk system, you could store your data base on either drive C or drive A. Your instructor might have some directions on which drive to use for your particular class. When you've highlighted the drive where you want your data base file to be stored, press **Enter** to select it.

Step 3: Name the Data Base File

Since every file must have a name, you need to name your data base. At this point, dBASE III PLUS should be prompting you to enter a name for your file (see Figure 3.6). The name of a data base file can have up to eight characters in it. Although the first character must be a letter of the alphabet, the remaining characters can be any combination of letters, digits, and underscores (_). A data base file name cannot contain spaces or any other symbols. When naming a file, you can type in either uppercase or lowercase letters, but dBASE stores them as uppercase. If you enter more than eight characters, dBASE ignores all but the first eight. As with all file names, the name should remind you of the file's contents. For our example mailing list data base, type **mailing** and press **Enter**.

Figure 3.6   Name the Data Base File

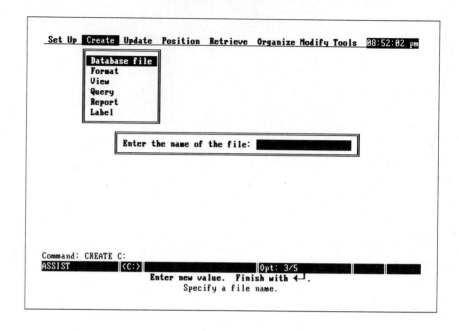

Step 4: Define the Fields

After you enter an acceptable name, dBASE III PLUS displays an empty data base file structure table. Your screen should look like Figure 3.7.

Figure 3.7   Empty Data Base Structure Table

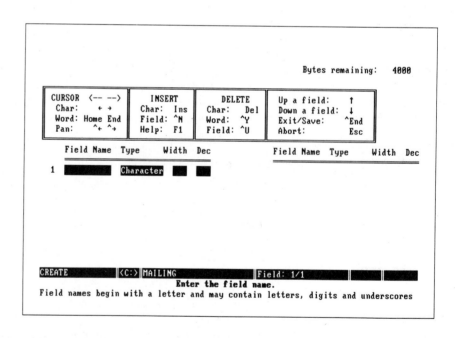

At this point you tell dBASE how to structure the records of your data base. Since the maximum length of a dBASE III PLUS record is 4,000 bytes, a message is displayed at the top right telling you how much room you have left for the record definition. As you add fields, the 4,000 will decrease. In practice, most data base records take up much less than 4,000 bytes.

The boxed-in area beneath the bytes-remaining message is a help menu that tells you how to move about and enter information. Beneath that is the empty table where you enter the name, type, and width of each field in your data base record. Finally, at the very bottom are the status bar, navigation line, and message line. Note how the status bar now reflects the name of the data base file you are working on and the field you are currently editing.

First, you must decide what fields to include in your data base; then for each field you have to choose its name, data type, and width. If the field is a numeric value, you must also decide the number of digits to appear to the right of the decimal point. Examine the Kwik Key & Lock mailing list in Figure 3.4. There are six fields: last name, first name, address, city, state, and ZIP code. Naming the fields after the contents is a good idea. More thought has to be applied to choosing field widths: you want to choose widths that aren't too big because that will waste storage space, yet you want the fields to be wide enough to hold the necessary information. Deciding on the data type for each field is pretty straightforward. dBASE III PLUS has five types of data fields:

Character   up to 254 letters, digits, and symbols
Numeric   numbers used in calculations
Date   dates of the form mm/dd/yy
Logical   True or False, Yes or No
Memo   free-form text for notes

The Kwik Key & Lock mailing list is a fairly simple example. All of its fields are character fields. Note that although the address and ZIP code fields contain numbers, those numbers are classified as text because they don't represent quantities and won't be used in calculations. The following names, types, and sizes might be appropriate for your mailing list data base structure:

Field Name	Type	Width
LAST_NAME	Character	15
FIRST_NAME	Character	10
ADDRESS	Character	20
CITY	Character	10
STATE	Character	5
ZIP	Character	5

Step 5: Enter the Definition

Once you've decided on the field names, types, and widths, you can enter them into the empty data base structure table. Field names can be up to ten characters long, the first of which must be a letter. Like file names, the remaining characters can be only letters, digits, or underscores. You can enter field names in uppercase or lowercase, but dBASE III PLUS will convert the characters to all uppercase. Type **LAST_NAME** and press **Enter**. The cursor will move to the data type column, which is already filled with Character. To change to another data type, you could enter its first letter or press the Space Bar to cycle through the possible selections. Since Character is what you want here, just press **Enter**. The cursor will move to the field width column. Type **15** and press **Enter**. You're done with the first field, so dBASE III PLUS will automatically drop down to let you specify the second field. Type **FIRST_NAME** and notice how dBASE beeps and moves the cursor to the data type column. When you completely fill the space for the field name, you don't have to press Enter because dBASE automatically goes on to the next specification. Enter the remaining field definitions. If you make a mistake, just use the arrow keys to move the cursor to the erroneous entry and retype it. You can also use the options listed up in the help box to move about, insert characters, and delete characters. When you're done defining the ZIP field, press **Enter**. Your screen should look like Figure 3.8.

Figure 3.8   Field Names Entered

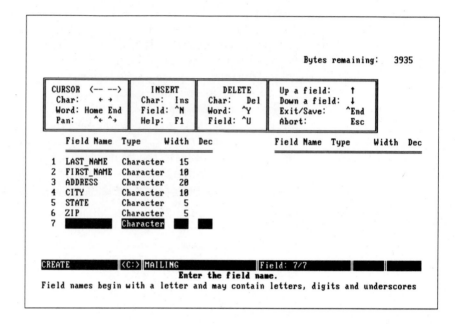

Step 6: Save the Data Base Structure

Recheck your work to make sure that the fields are defined correctly. When you're sure that everything is correct, hold down **Control** and press **End**. This procedure tells dBASE that you're done defining your data base. The message line will say:

Press ENTER to confirm. Any other key to resume.

Press **Enter** and dBASE III PLUS will save your data base structure. It will then ask you if you want to go ahead and input your data records now. Since that's our next lesson, press **Y**. If you press **N**, you'll be returned to the Assistant menu.

Lesson 4: Entering Data Base Records

All you've done so far is define the structure of a new data base; it doesn't have any data in it yet. You now face the somewhat tedious task of keying in your data.

Step 1: Examine the Data Entry Form

Your screen should now display a blank template, or data entry form, that looks like Figure 3.9.

The boxed-in area at the top is a help menu like the one you saw when you created the data base structure. It lists the keys you need to press to move about, enter, and correct record fields. Along the left side is a list of the names of the fields in each record of this data base. The reverse video block to the right of each field name is where you will type in the data for that field. The width of the block shows the width of the field as you specified it. The cursor initially is placed at the first character of the first field of the first record.

Figure 3.9   Blank Data Entry
Form

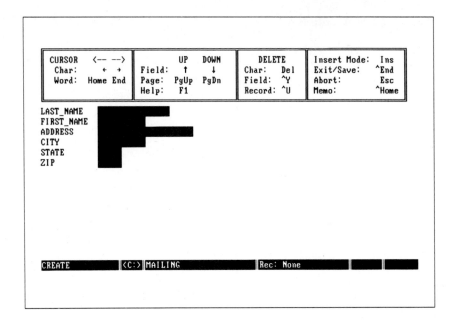

Step 2: Enter the Records

Refer to the Kwik Key & Lock mailing list in Figure 3.4. To enter the first field of
the first record, type **Abel** and press **Enter**. The cursor will drop down to the
FIRST_NAME field. Now enter **Larry** for the first name, **906 Busey #5** for the
address, **Urbana** for the city, and **IL** for the state. Type **61801** for the ZIP code,
but don't press Enter after it. Don't be alarmed when dBASE beeps and seemingly
erases what you've just typed. Because the ZIP field is five characters wide and
you've typed exactly five characters, dBASE automatically enters that field, stores
the record, goes on to the next record, and beeps to signal what it's done. This feature is handy for entering records one after another, but it requires you to go back
and view a record again if you want to check its accuracy. To do this, just press
the **Up Arrow** key or the **PgUp** key to return to a previously entered record (see
Figure 3.10). Use the **PgDn** key to proceed to the next blank data entry form to
continue entering records.

Now input the rest of the records from the Kwik Key & Lock mailing list. Notice how the status bar changes each time you enter a new record or move to a
previous one. For example, when you enter the second record, it will say *Rec:*
EOF/1. This message means that the data base currently has one record in it and
you are entering a new record at the end of file (EOF).

Step 3: Terminate Data Entry

As you input each record, dBASE III PLUS adds it to your data base file. When
you are finished entering the records, press **Ctrl-End** to terminate the data entry
process. Your data base will be saved on disk and you will be returned to the
Create/Database file submenu option from which you started.

**Figure 3.10   A Data Base
Record**

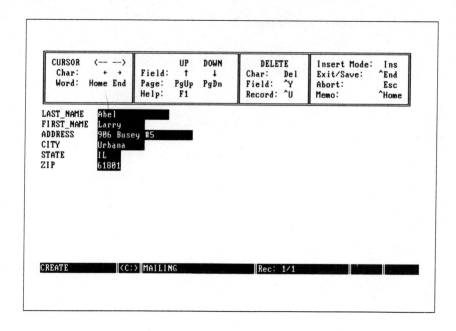

Lesson 5: Examining an Existing Data Base

Now that you've got a complete data base, you'd probably like to take a look at it.
One of the major advantages of a data base program is the flexibility with which
you can retrieve previously stored information. There are a great many different
ways to access a data base with dBASE III PLUS. In this lesson we'll look at a few
simple methods that work well with small data bases like your mailing list
example.

Step 1: Select the Data Base

The first thing you must do before you can work with an existing data base is tell
dBASE what file to use. This step is accomplished through the Set Up option. Use
the **Left** or **Right Arrow** key to move the menu bar highlight block to Set Up.
The submenu highlight block should be on top of the Database file option. Press
Enter and dBASE will display its disk drive submenu. Select the drive where your
copy of the mailing list data base is stored and press **Enter**. A list of data base
files on the disk in the drive you selected will pop up next. MAILING.DBF should
be in that list as shown in Figure 3.11. Position the highlight block on it and press
Enter. You'll then be asked:

        Is the file indexed? [Y/N]

Here dBASE is trying to find out if this data has been rearranged with the index
command. You'll learn more about indexing in a later lesson. For now, just press
N for no. MAILING.DBF will be selected as the current data base file with which
to work and you'll be returned to the Set Up submenu.

Figure 3.11   List of Data Base Files

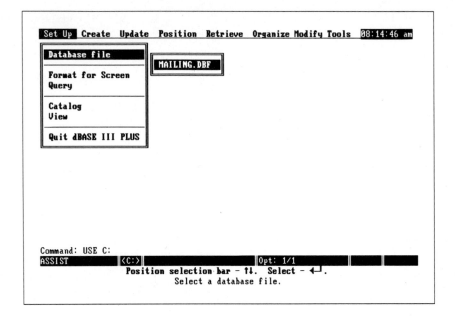

Step 2: List the Data Base Structure

When examining a data base you've never seen before or one that you haven't worked with for awhile, you'll probably want to take a look at the record structure. The Assistant's Tools option offers you this opportunity. Move the highlight block to the Tools option with the **Left** or **Right Arrow** key. Use the **Down Arrow** key to select the List structure option and press **Enter**. You'll then be asked:

```
Direct the output to the printer? [Y/N]
```

Press **N** if you don't want a copy of the data base structure sent to your printer. Your screen should look like Figure 3.12.

Figure 3.12   Data Base Structure

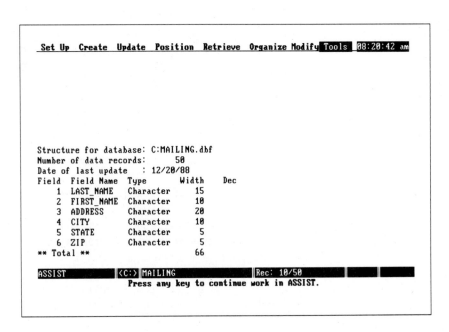

When you're done examining the structure listing, press any key to return to the Assistant menu.

Step 3: Browse through the Data Base

If your data base is fairly small, and there are no particular records you want to look at, the easiest thing to do is browse. Select the Update option of the Assistant's menu bar with the **Left** or **Right Arrow** key. Use the **Down Arrow** key to select the Browse submenu option and press **Enter**. Figure 3.13 shows what you'll see.

Figure 3.13   The Browse Option

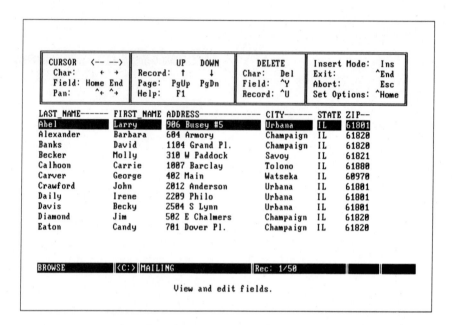

Use the **PgDn** key to look at the next page of records and use **PgUp** to look at the previous page. Note that this option can also be used to modify data base records; we'll have more to say about this function shortly. For now, just browse through the table of mailing list records. When you're done, press **Ctrl-End** or **Escape** to return to the Assistant menu.

Step 4: Retrieve and Display Data Base Records

Another way to look at a data base is with the Retrieve option. Although this option is not quite as easy to use as browsing for looking at all of a small data base, it still does the job. Select the Retrieve option from the Assistant menu. Use the **Down Arrow** to highlight the Display submenu option and press **Enter**. Select the Specify scope option of the new submenu that pops up. One more submenu will pop up. Select the ALL option to display the entire data base (see Figure 3.14). Now select the Execute the command option and press **Enter**. The data base records will be displayed a page at a time, as shown in Figure 3.15. To see the next page, press any key when prompted to do so. Unfortunately, there's no way to go back to a previously displayed page. When the last page of records has been displayed, press any key to return to the Assistant menu.

Figure 3.14   The Display Option

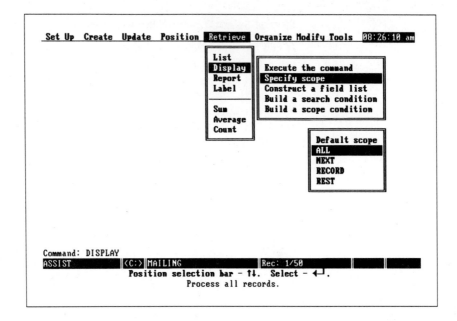

Figure 3.15   The All Option

```
   Set Up  Create  Update  Position  Retrieve  Organize Modify Tools   08:26:19 am

Record#  LAST_NAME   FIRST_NAME ADDRESS          CITY       STATE ZIP
      1  Abel        Larry      986 Busey #5     Urbana     IL    61801
      2  Alexander   Barbara    604 Armory       Champaign  IL    61820
      3  Banks       David      1104 Grand Pl.   Champaign  IL    61820
      4  Becker      Molly      310 W Paddock    Savoy      IL    61821
      5  Calhoon     Carrie     1007 Barclay     Tolono     IL    61880
      6  Carver      George     402 Main         Watseka    IL    60970
      7  Crawford    John       2012 Anderson    Urbana     IL    61801
      8  Daily       Irene      2209 Philo       Urbana     IL    61801
      9  Davis       Becky      2504 S Lynn      Urbana     IL    61801
     10  Diamond     Jim        502 E Chalmers   Champaign  IL    61820
     11  Eaton       Candy      701 Dover Pl.    Champaign  IL    61820
     12  Edwards     Barbara    1721 Valley Rd   Paxton     IL    60957
     13  Feldman     Francis    809 W Elm        Urbana     IL    61801
     14  Franklin    Melissa    566 W Church     Champaign  IL    61820
     15  Garret      Gerald     1871 Parkdale    Rantoul    IL    61866
     16  Griffith    Oscar      805 W Florida    Urbana     IL    61801
     17  Hall        Robert     102 White        Pekin      IL    61554
Press any key to continue...
ASSIST            <C:> MAILING                  Rec: 1/50
```

Lesson 6: Adding New Records

Most data bases are very dynamic entities; they're constantly being changed as people use them. For example, as Kwik Key & Lock gains more customers, new records will have to be added to its mailing list data base. Appending new records is one of the most frequently used data base operations.

Step 1: Select the Data Base

If you haven't already selected the data base to which you want to add, you have to tell dBASE what file to use. This step is exactly the same procedure that you did in Step 1 of Lesson 5. Unless you've exited dBASE or selected a different file since you did the last lesson, MAILING.DBF should still be the current data base and you don't have to do anything for this step. Check the status bar to make sure that MAILING is selected. From now on, unless we indicate otherwise, we'll assume that you've selected this mailing list data base.

Step 2: Select the Append Option

Appending records to an existing data base is very similar to entering records to a newly created data base. From the Assistant's main menu bar, use the **Left** or **Right Arrow** key to move the highlight block to the Update option. The Append option should be highlighted, so just press **Enter** (see Figure 3.16).

Figure 3.16   The Append Option

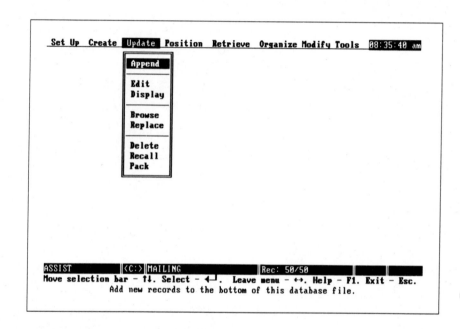

Step 3: Enter the Record

Your screen should now display the same data entry form you saw when entering records. The screen should look like Figure 3.9, except that the status bar will list *Rec: EOF/50* as the current record. This designation means that you have fifty records in the file and you're about to enter number 51. Enter the following record:

Robinson
James
2458 W Michigan
Champaign
IL
61821

Step 4: Terminate Data Entry

As soon as you finish typing the ZIP code, dBASE will beep and store the record. A blank data entry form for the next record (number 52) will pop up. If you had more than one new record to add, you could just continue entering them. Press **Ctrl-End** to terminate data entry and dBASE will return to the Assistant's Update submenu.

Lesson 7: Modifying Existing Records

What if one of Kwik Key & Lock's customers moves? His or her record will have to be modified to reflect the change of address. Updating the contents of existing records is another very common data base operation.

Step 1: Select the Record

Just as dBASE remembers the data base file on which you're currently working, it also keeps track of the record. Whenever you are using a data base, an invisible pointer is always pointing to a particular record. This current record is the one that's listed in the status bar after the Rec:. The number before the slash is the current record, and the number after it is the total number of records in the data base.

If you know the number of the record you want to modify, you can tell dBASE to point to it as the current record. Use the **Left** or **Right Arrow** key to move the highlight block to the Assistant's Position option. Press the **Up** or **Down Arrow** key until the submenu highlight block is on top of the Goto Record option. Press **Enter** and dBASE will display another submenu with three choices: TOP, BOTTOM, and RECORD (see Figure 3.17). If you want the very first record in the

Figure 3.17   Select a Record

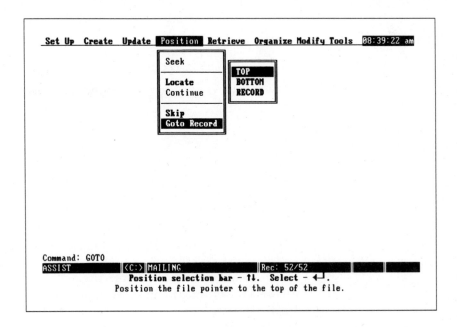

data base, you'd select TOP. If you want the very last record in the data base, you'd select BOTTOM. To select a particular record number, move the highlight block to the RECORD and press **Enter**. Do this now. As you can see, the program asks you to:

    Enter a numeric value:

Here dBASE is prompting you for the number of the record you want to select as the current record. Type **51** and press **Enter** to select the new record you just appended in Lesson 6. Note that in this particular case, you could also have used the BOTTOM option. The status bar will now say Rec: 51/51 and dBASE will return to the Position submenu of the Assistant menu.

Step 2: Select the Edit Option

Press the **Left Arrow** key to move the highlight block back to the Update option. Use the **Down Arrow** key to select the Edit option and press **Enter**. Figure 3.18 shows what you should see on your screen.

Figure 3.18   The Edit Option

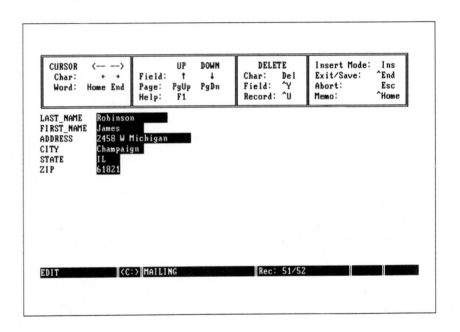

Step 3: Make the Correction

Now that the current record is displayed on your screen, you're free to move the cursor about within the fields and make any corrections. Press the **Down Arrow** key twice to move the cursor to the address field. Type **610 N Duncan** and press the **Del** key three times to overwrite and delete the rest of the 2458 W Michigan. To exit the edit mode and save the modification to the data base file, press **Ctrl-End**.

Step 4: Use the Browse Option

As with most dBASE III PLUS operations, there are several ways to modify existing records. One way is with the Update/Edit option as you've just done. Another way is to use the Update/Browse option. This alternative can be a little easier to use if your data base is fairly short and you don't know the exact number of the record you need to change.

You should be looking at the Update submenu. Use the **Down Arrow** key to select the Browse option and press **Enter**. Since the current record is still the last one in the data base, you'll see the highlight bar positioned on James Robinson's record. Press the **Up Arrow** key to see how Browse lets you move through the data base. You can modify any record selected with the highlight bar by simply moving the cursor within the record, and overwriting, inserting, and deleting characters. When you're done, press **Ctrl-End** to save your modifications and return to the Assistant menu.

Lesson 8: Deleting Records

Occasionally, records must be completely removed from a data base. In the Kwik Key & Lock example, customers might move far away or even die, their accounts might become inactive, they might switch locksmiths, or they simply might not want to receive ads in the mail. From time to time the mailing list data base will have to be purged of these unused records.

Step 1: Select the Record

As we've said before, if you know a record's number, selecting it is easy. In most cases, however, you probably won't know the number of the record to be selected. You'll want to select it on the basis of what's in one or more fields. For example, you'd know the name of the customer whose record is to be deleted. In the next lesson we'll show you how to select records on the basis of field contents. To simplify matters for the moment, let's assume you do know the record number. Use the Position option to select record number 51 just like you did in Step 1 of Lesson 7.

Step 2: Select the Delete Option

Once you've positioned the current record pointer to the record you want to remove, deleting it is easy. Use the **Left** or **Right Arrow** key to select the Update option. Now use the **Down Arrow** key to move the submenu highlight block on top of the Delete option and press **Enter**. Another submenu will pop up with its highlight block on the option entitled Execute the command (see Figure 3.19). Press **Enter** to execute the delete command. You'll be informed that one record was deleted and the message line will tell you to press any key to go back to the Assistant menu.

If you now execute the Browse option, you'll see that Mr. Robinson's record is still there. What's going on here? As an extra safety feature and also because of the way records are stored by dBASE III PLUS, deleting a record does not immediately remove it from storage. It's only invisibly marked as a deleted record. You can still get it back into your data base again with the Recall option of the Update submenu.

Figure 3.19   The Delete Option

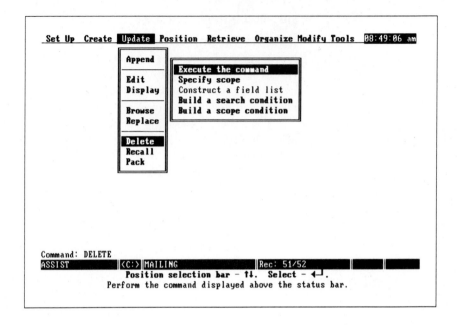

Step 3: Pack the Data Base

To remove deleted records permanently, you must use the Pack option of the Update submenu. This operation removes all records marked for deletion and renumbers the remaining records. Once you do a Pack, you can't get back deleted records with Recall. So, be sure you really want to remove your deleted records before you select the Pack option. Use the **Down Arrow** key to position the highlight block on top of Pack and press **Enter**. dBASE will check through all the records of your data base and keep only the ones that haven't been marked for deletion. It will tell you how many records were "copied" (i.e., kept), and you'll be told to press any key to continue work in the Assistant menu. Now do a Browse again. You'll see that Mr. Robinson's data, record number 51, is really gone.

Lesson 9: Searching For Records

As we said in the last lesson, most of the time you won't remember a particular record's number. If you want to display, print, modify, or delete a particular record, you must somehow locate it within the data base. Other times, you might want to find several records that fulfill certain criteria. For example, you might want to see the records of all customers that live in Urbana. Sometimes you'd like to combine criteria: all the customers whose last names begin with D who live in Urbana. As you can imagine, the larger your data base and the greater the number of fields, the more complex your searches can be. dBASE III PLUS has many ways to search for records within data bases. In this lesson we'll cover a few of the simplest methods.

Step 1: Locate a Particular Record

Frequently, you'd like to be able to locate a particular record within a data base. You might want to modify, delete, or simply display one specific record. For example, let's say that you know Ellen McFall is a customer and you want to see her

record. Since she's probably the only one in the data base named McFall, searching on the basis of her last name would be a good place to start.

If you just want to display her record, you could use the Retrieve option of the
Assistant menu.   Select the Display option of the Retrieve submenu and press
Enter. You'll see a new submenu that has five options. Select the second option,
Specify scope. This option will bring up another menu that lets you tell dBASE
through what portion of the data base you want it to search. Select ALL and press
Enter; the Specify scope submenu will disappear. Now use the **Down Arrow** key
to select the Build a search condition option and press **Enter**. A menu of the
record fields of the mailing list data base will appear. Press **Enter** to select
LAST_NAME. A menu of comparison operators will appear on your screen. Select
the = Equal to option and press **Enter**. dBASE will ask you to:

```
Enter a character string (without quotes):
```

Here the program is asking for the last name you want to search for, so type
McFall and press **Enter** (see Figure 3.20). Yet another little submenu will pop up
with options for combining search criteria. Since we're searching only on the basis
of last name in this example, just press **Enter** to select the No more conditions option. Now select Execute the command and press **Enter**. dBASE will retrieve and
display Ellen McFall's record in a single row above the status bar, as shown in
Figure 3.21. Note that it lists the record number as 29, but it doesn't change the
current record number in the status bar.

If you want to modify or delete Ellen McFall's record, you'd still have to use
the Assistant's Position option. Since you now know her record number, you could
use the Go to Record submenu option to make record number 29 the current
record. If you knew that you wanted to modify or delete her record from the start,
you could use the Locate option of the Position submenu instead of the Display option of the Retrieve submenu. This method wouldn't display her record, but it
would establish her record as the current record. Then you could execute an Edit
or Delete from the Update submenu.

Figure 3.20   Character String
Entered

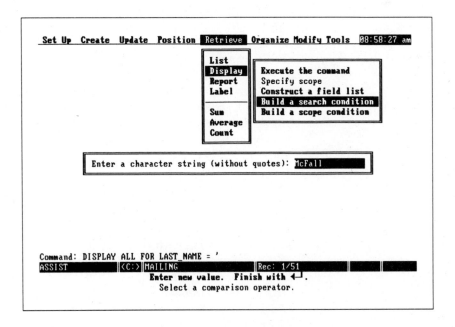

**Figure 3.21   Data Base
Record Retrieved**

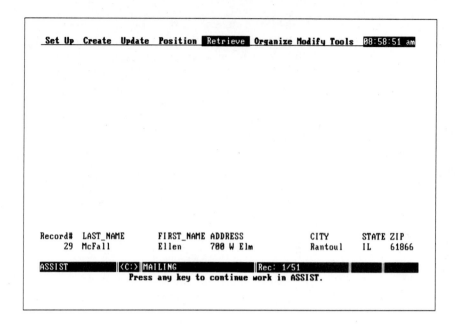

Step 2: Display Several Records

Let's say that you want to see the records of all customers who live in Urbana.
The procedure for finding multiple records is just as easy as finding a single record.
Go back to the Retrieve option of the Assistant menu.   Select the Display submenu
option.   Select ALL from the Specify scope option.   Now select Build a search
condition.   This time, instead of choosing the LAST_NAME field, select CITY and
press **Enter**.   Choose the = Equal to comparison condition and enter **Urbana** for
the character string to search for.   Select No more conditions.   Before you go ahead
and execute this search, examine the action line right above the status bar.   It says:

```
Command: DISPLAY ALL FOR CITY = 'Urbana'
```

This is the dot-prompt command that corresponds to all the menu selecting you've
just done.   In other words, if you press **Escape** from The Assistant to get to the
dBASE command mode, this command is what you'd have to enter to search for
the Urbana records.   Perhaps you can begin to see why some people, as they become more experienced, prefer commands to menus.

Finally, select Execute the command to complete the search.   dBASE III PLUS
will extract all those records with *Urbana* in the city field and display them in a
table on your screen.   Figure 3.22 shows what you should see.

Step 3: Use Multiple Conditions

There are times when you might want to search for records on the basis of more
complex criteria.   Let's say that you wanted to display the records of customers
whose names begin with *D* and who live in Urbana .   Repeat what you did in Step 2
up to the point you select the No more conditions option of the Build a search condition submenu.   This time, select the Combine with .AND. option and press
Enter.   The submenu of record fields will pop up again and this time select
LAST_NAME.   From the menu of comparisons, pick >= Greater Than or Equal
To and press **Enter**.   Enter **D** for the character string to compare to.   Now again
choose Combine with .AND. and select LAST_NAME.   This time, however, choose

**Figure 3.22   All Records with
Urbana in the City Field**

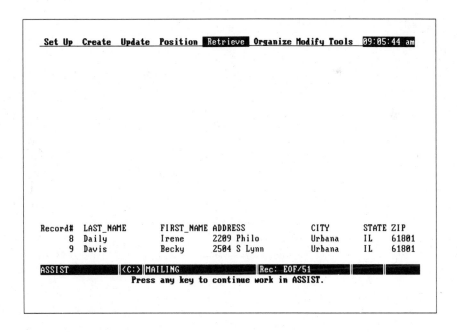

```
   Set Up  Create  Update  Position  █Retrieve█  Organize Modify Tools   09:02:57 am



   Record#  LAST_NAME    FIRST_NAME ADDRESS              CITY     STATE ZIP
         1  Abel         Larry      906 Busey #5         Urbana   IL    61801
         7  Crawford     John       2012 Anderson        Urbana   IL    61801
         8  Daily        Irene      2209 Philo           Urbana   IL    61801
         9  Davis        Becky      2504 S Lynn          Urbana   IL    61801
        13  Feldman      Francis    809 W Elm            Urbana   IL    61801
        16  Griffith     Oscar      805 W Florida        Urbana   IL    61801
        19  Irving       Judith     1904 Oliver Dr       Urbana   IL    61801
        27  Lowrey       Marcy      407 W Coler          Urbana   IL    61801
        30  Mitchell     Dan        909 Crestwood        Urbana   IL    61801
        32  Novak        Sandy      3008 Kyle            Urbana   IL    61801
        38  Reeves       Mike       1507 S Race          Urbana   IL    61801
        39  Ressel       Ruby       124 W Park           Urbana   IL    61801
        42  Spencer      Linda      506 E Oregon         Urbana   IL    61801
        45  Underwood    Rhonda     1243 W Green         Urbana   IL    61801
        47  Walden       Roxanne    134 Doddson          Urbana   IL    61801

   ASSIST         <C:> MAILING                   Rec: EOF/51
                   Press any key to continue work in ASSIST.
```

the < Less Than option and enter E as the character string to compare to. Finally, select No more conditions and then Execute the command. You should see Irene Daily and Becky Davis's records displayed on your screen, as shown in Figure 3.23.

**Figure 3.23   Irene Daily and
Becky Davis's Records**

```
   Set Up  Create  Update  Position  █Retrieve█  Organize Modify Tools   09:05:44 am









   Record#  LAST_NAME    FIRST_NAME ADDRESS              CITY     STATE ZIP
         8  Daily        Irene      2209 Philo           Urbana   IL    61801
         9  Davis        Becky      2504 S Lynn          Urbana   IL    61801
   ASSIST         <C:> MAILING                   Rec: EOF/51
                   Press any key to continue work in ASSIST.
```

With all the menu selections you've made to accomplish this search, you might be a bit confused about what you've just done. As you should know by now, when dealing with computers, you have to tell them *exactly* what to do. Quite literally, you've told dBASE to display every record whose city field is equal to *Urbana*, and whose last name field is greater than or equal to *D* and less than *E*. These greater than and less than comparisons are how dBASE "knows" a last name begins with *D*. Letters of the alphabet are encoded by computers as numeric values that increase in magnitude as you approach *Z*. So, $A < B < C < \ldots < Z$. Names that begin with *D* are "less than" names that begin with *E*.

Lesson 10: Global Updating

Sometimes it's useful to be able to go through an entire data base and make changes or delete selected records. Such operations are called "global" because they are applied everywhere—that is, every record in the data base is checked. For example, let's say that the fair city of Champaign, Illinois, duly voted to change its name to Shampoo and you wanted to update the Kwik Key & Lock mailing list to reflect the new name. You could, of course, use Browse to go through every record and change each *Champaign* you find to *Shampoo*. This approach, however, would be a tiresome task, and dBASE III PLUS provides a much easier, quicker, and more accurate method.

Step 1: Select the Replace Option

Use the **Left** or **Right Arrow** key to move the highlight block to the Assistant's Update option. Now use the **Up** or **Down Arrow** key to select Replace and press **Enter**.

Step 2: Select the Field

You should now see on the right side of your screen a submenu of record fields (see Figure 3.24). Use the **Down Arrow** key to highlight CITY and press **Enter**.

Figure 3.24   Record Fields Submenu

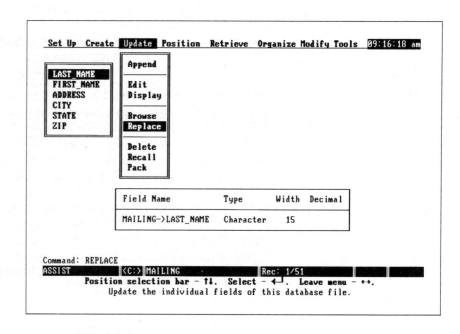

Step 3: Enter the New Field Contents

At this point dBASE is asking you to:

        Enter a character string (without quotes):

You're being prompted to enter what you want the contents of the city field to be changed to. Type **Shampoo** and press **Enter**. dBASE will put up the field menu again, but since you're changing only one field this time, just press the **Left** or **Right Arrow** key to leave this menu.

Step 4: Specify the Scope

Just as you saw in the last lesson, a submenu will pop up with the options for specifying what to search for and which records to search. Select the Specify scope option and then pick ALL to apply the search throughout the entire data base.

Step 5: Execute the Search and Replace

Now select the option entitled Build a search condition. Select the CITY field again, choose the = Equal to condition, and enter **Champaign** as the character string to search for. Finally, select No more conditions and then Execute the command. dBASE will say how many records were replaced and then tell you to press any key to return to The Assistant.

Step 6: Examine the Data Base

Use the Browse option of The Assistant's Update submenu to take a look at your mailing list. Sure enough, every *Champaign* has been replaced with *Shampoo*, as shown in Figure 3.25.

Figure 3.25   All Occurences of Champaign Replaced with Shampoo

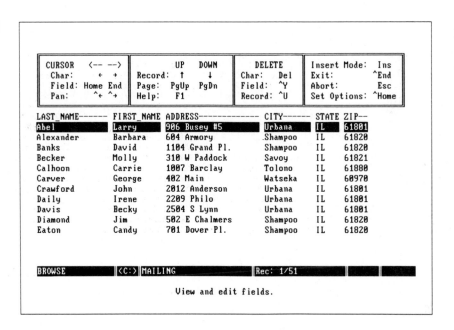

Step 7: Select the Delete Option

The global deletion of selected records operates similarly to global replacement. For example, you could decide that Champaign/Shampoo residents are just too silly and delete them outright from the Kwik Key & Lock mailing list. To do this, use the **Up** or **Down Arrow** key to highlight the Delete option of the Update submenu. Specify the scope to be ALL and then build the search condition. This time the field you're searching is CITY, the comparison is = Equal to, and the character string to search for is *Shampoo*. When you execute the command, dBASE will inform you that sixteen records were deleted. Press any key to return to The Assistant.

Step 8: Recall the Deleted Records

We were only kidding about deleting all those Champaign/Shampoo residents. Fortunately, because you haven't packed the data base, you can get all the deleted records back again with the Recall option of the Update submenu. Use the **Up** or **Down Arrow** key to highlight Recall and press **Enter**. Specify the scope to be ALL and then execute the command. dBASE will say that sixteen records were recalled and tell you to press any key to go back to The Assistant. Now use the Replace option again to change every *Shampoo* back to *Champaign*.

Lesson 11: Modifying the Data Base Structure

Occasionally, you need to change the structure of an existing data base. You might have to change the name, type, or length of a field; add new fields; or delete existing fields. dBASE III PLUS lets you do all these things.

Step 1: Make Sure There's Room

When you change the structure of an existing data base, dBASE III PLUS first has to make a temporary copy of the whole thing. So, you have to make sure there's room for a complete copy of your existing data base file on whichever disk it's stored. That shouldn't be a problem with your relatively small mailing list data base. However, we'll show you how to check anyway, just to be on the safe side.

Use the **Left** or **Right Arrow** key to move the highlight block to the Tools option of the Assistant menu and press **Enter**. Select the Directory submenu option and press **Enter**. Now choose the letter of the disk drive on which your data base file is stored. Finally, select the option .dbf Database Files to list only data base files (see Figure 3.26). dBASE will display the data base files, how much room they all take up, and how much room is left on the disk. If there's only one data base file on your disk, you can easily ensure that there's enough room for a copy: the number of bytes in the file should be less than the number of bytes remaining. Press any key to return to the Assistant menu.

Step 2: Modify a Field Name

Move the highlight block to The Assistant's Modify option and press **Enter**. Select the Database file submenu option and press **Enter**. The data base structure table on your screen should look similar to Figure 3.8. Use the **Down Arrow** key to move the highlight block down to the ZIP code field. Instead of just ZIP, change the field name to **ZIP_CODE**. Press **Ctrl-End** to save the new data base structure. You'll be asked:

```
Should data be COPIED from backup for all fields? (Y/N)
```

Be sure that you answer **Y** for yes. If you don't, the ZIP codes won't be copied from the temporary file. Press **Enter** to confirm the new data base structure.

Figure 3.26   List Data Base Files from the Directory Submenu

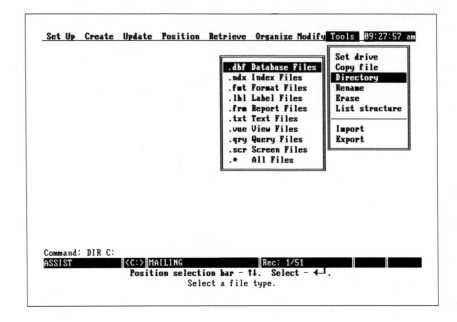

Step 3: Modify a Field Length

You should still be in the Modify submenu. Press **Enter** to choose the Database file option again. The new data base structure table should appear on your screen. Note that the ZIP code field is now named ZIP_CODE.

You might have noticed that we originally told you to set the width of the STATE field to 5, but the state abbreviations are all only two letters. This discrepancy wastes three bytes per record. Although this loss might not seem like much, it could add up to a significant waste of disk space if the data base grows very large. Move the cursor to the width column of the STATE field and change the 5 to a 2.

Step 4: Add New Fields

As an example, let's add two new fields to your existing Kwik Key & Lock mailing list data base. These fields will be numeric fields containing each customer's balance (how much they paid) for the first and second halves of 1989. You'll end up with a data base that will tell you how much business Kwik Key & Lock received from each of its customers for the first and second halves of the year. Later we'll see how dBASE III PLUS can do calculations on numeric fields, compute totals, and include these in a data base report.

Use the **Down Arrow** key to move the highlight block below the ZIP code field. A new blank field will be generated. Type **BALANCE_1** and press **Enter**. The cursor will jump to the data type column, which now says *Character*. Press the **Space Bar** once to change the *Character* to *Numeric* and press **Enter**. For the field width, type **10** and press **Enter**. Finally, enter **2** for the number of decimal places. Now enter the second new field just like the first, but call this one BALANCE_2. Your screen should look like Figue 3.27. Press **Ctrl-End** to save the new data base structure and press **Enter** when asked to confirm the change.

Figure 3.27   New Fields Added to Data Base File

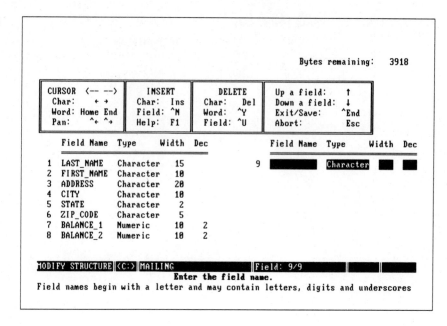

Step 5: Add New Field Contents

Select the Browse option of the Assistant's Update submenu to examine your modified data base. Move to the beginning of the file by using the **PgUp** key. Notice that the STATE field is now only two characters wide and the name of the ZIP code field is ZIP_CODE. So far, so good, but where are the new fields? They won't fit on the screen, so you have to pan right to see them. Look up in the help menu under CURSOR. At the bottom next to *Pan*, the menu tells you how to shift the screen sideways. Hold down **Control** and press the **Right Arrow** key to see the two new fields. They're ten columns wide and the decimal point is in the right place, but the fields are empty, as shown in Figure 3.28.

Figure 3.28   View and Edit Fields

```
┌─────────────────────────────────────────────────────────────────────────┐
│  CURSOR   <── ──>              UP   DOWN        DELETE      Insert Mode: Ins│
│  Char:        ← →   Record:   ↑    ↓       Char:   Del   Exit:     ^End   │
│  Field: Home End    Page:  PgUp  PgDn      Field:  ^Y    Abort:     Esc    │
│  Pan:     ^← ^→     Help:   F1             Record: ^U    Set Options: ^Home│
│                                                                           │
│ FIRST_NAME ADDRESS───────────── CITY────── STATE ZIP_CODE BALANCE_1─ BALANCE_2─│
│ Larry      906 Busey #5         Urbana     IL    61801                     │
│ Barbara    604 Armory           Champaign  IL    61820       .         .   │
│ David      1104 Grand Pl.       Champaign  IL    61820       .         .   │
│ Molly      310 W Paddock        Savoy      IL    61821       .         .   │
│ Carrie     1007 Barclay         Tolono     IL    61880       .         .   │
│ George     402 Main             Watseka    IL    60970       .         .   │
│ John       2012 Anderson        Urbana     IL    61801       .         .   │
│ Irene      2209 Philo           Urbana     IL    61801       .         .   │
│ Becky      2504 S Lynn          Urbana     IL    61801       .         .   │
│ Jim        502 E Chalmers       Champaign  IL    61820       .         .   │
│ Candy      701 Dover Pl.        Champaign  IL    61820       .         .   │
│                                                                           │
│ BROWSE         |<C:>|MAILING                   |Rec: 1/51                  │
│                          View and edit fields.                            │
└─────────────────────────────────────────────────────────────────────────┘
```

Use The Assistant's Position option to make sure the current record pointer is at the beginning of the data base file. Move The Assistant's highlight block to Update and then select the Edit submenu option. Press **Enter** and the data entry form for record number 1 will appear on your screen. Note that the balance fields are empty. Use the **Down Arrow** key to move the cursor to the BALANCE_1 field, type **25.50**, and press **Enter**. See how the number automatically adjusts to fit into the field. Now enter 10.25 for field BALANCE_2. dBASE will automatically advance to the next record so that you can edit it.

Now enter the BALANCE_1 and BALANCE_2 figures from the following table for the remaining records, 2 through 50. When you are finished, press **Ctrl-End** to save your updated data base and return to the Assistant menu.

RECORD	BALANCE_1	BALANCE_2	RECORD	BALANCE_1	BALANCE_2
2	52.00	25.75	26	10.25	25.50
3	84.25	22.75	27	25.75	52.00
4	12.25	58.00	28	22.75	84.25
5	23.50	14.50	29	58.00	12.25
6	90.50	30.50	30	14.50	23.50
7	0.00	25.50	31	30.50	90.50
8	45.00	54.25	32	25.50	0.00
9	78.50	24.75	33	54.25	45.00
10	89.00	15.40	34	24.75	78.50
11	92.83	82.54	35	15.40	89.00
12	92.95	123.00	36	82.54	92.83
13	29.23	98.23	37	123.00	92.95
14	15.32	44.56	38	98.23	29.23
15	25.84	72.33	39	44.56	15.32
16	34.54	25.65	40	72.33	25.84
17	22.33	52.41	41	25.65	34.54
18	43.88	23.43	42	52.41	22.33
19	22.55	43.22	43	23.43	43.88
20	38.22	41.55	44	43.22	22.55
21	22.11	51.37	45	41.55	38.22
22	21.54	43.64	46	51.37	22.11
23	25.00	0.00	47	43.64	21.54
24	10.50	45.99	48	0.00	25.00
25	52.75	23.53	49	45.99	10.50
			50	23.53	52.75

Lesson 12: Generating Reports

You've seen how to use the Browse and Display options to examine all or part of a data base on your screen. It's very common, however, to want a hard copy listing of the contents of a data base. These listings, or reports as they're usually called, can be generated by dBASE III PLUS according to instructions you provide. Furthermore, you have a great deal of flexibility in specifying the layout of a report. You can indicate the fields to include, the order in which they're to appear, where to put them, their headings, and whether to sum numeric fields. Once you set up a report layout, it can be saved in a disk file so that you can use it again in the future without having to respecify everything.

Step 1: Design the Report Layout

Let's say that it's the end of the year and you want a report for the Kwik Key & Lock customer balances. You don't need all the information in the data base–just first name, last name, city, both balances, and the total balance for each customer. In addition, you'd like a grand total of all the customer balances. Even though these balance totals aren't actually stored in your data base, dBASE III PLUS has the ability to do calculations on existing fields. The results of these calculations can easily be included in your report. At the top of each page you'd like a title, and at the top of each field column there should be a brief heading. dBASE III PLUS will automatically put the date and page number in the upper-left corner of each page.

Step 2: Create the Report Layout

Use the **Left** or **Right Arrow** key to move the highlight block to The Assistant's Create option. Select the Report submenu option and press **Enter**. Now select the disk drive on which you want your report layout file stored (you probably want it on the same disk as your data base files). dBASE III PLUS will ask you to:

    Enter the name of the file:

Here the program is asking you to choose a name for your report layout file. Type **BALANCE** and press **Enter**. dBASE will append .FRM as an extension to the name you choose. Your screen should now look like Figure 3.29.

Figure 3.29   Report Layout Parameters

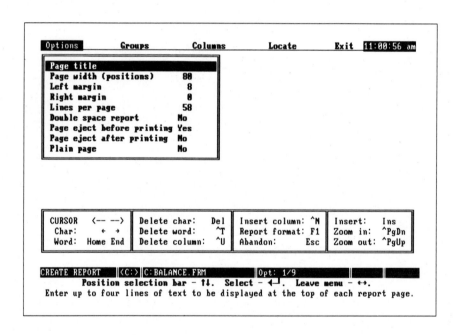

This first screen is where you set up the global layout for each page. As you can see, dBASE has already supplied default values for most settings. Press **Enter** to specify the title you want at the top of each page. A box will pop up on the right side of your screen. Here you can type up to four lines of text to be displayed at the top of each report page. Type **Kwik Key & Lock Customer Balances** and press **Ctrl-End**. Press the **Down Arrow** key twice and then press **Enter** to specify the left margin. Type **5** and press **Enter**. Now press the **Down Arrow** four times and then press **Enter** to turn off the page eject before printing. This procedure will save paper by not skipping to the top of a new page before printing your report. Just make sure that your printer is aligned to the top of a new page.

If you look closely, you can see that across the very top of your screen is a menu bar. You've just finished specifying the Options, so press the **Right Arrow** key twice to select the Columns submenu. We've skipped over the Groups option because there's no need to specify groups to subtotal. At the top of your screen you see a submenu where you will specify each field column that's to be in your report. Below is a representation of your report layout so far. Press **Enter** to specify the first column's contents. Now type **first_name** and press **Enter**. Press the **Down Arrow** once to highlight Heading and press **Enter**. Type **First Name** and press **Ctrl-End** to specify the first column's heading. The width is already specified by default, and dBASE will automatically leave one space between field columns. These settings are fine for this report. Your screen should look like Figure 3.30.

Now press **PgDn** to supply the contents of the next report column. Enter **last_name** for the contents and Last Name for the heading. Remember to press **Ctrl-End**, not Enter, when you're finished typing a heading. Notice the report format representation below. The five > symbols show the left margin you set to 5. The top line shows the headings you've specified, and the Xs down below show the field column widths. The dashes at the top show how much room you have left across the page.

Press **PgDn** again to specify the next column. Enter **city** for the contents, and **City** for the heading. Press **PgDn** to specify the first column of balances. Enter **balance_1** for the contents and **Balance 1** for the heading. Notice how the width and decimal places are set and how they appear down below in the report layout image. Since you do want your numeric columns totaled, leave the Total this column option set to *Yes*. Press **PgDn** and set up the next column for the second balance.

Figure 3.30   Report Format for BALANCE.FRM

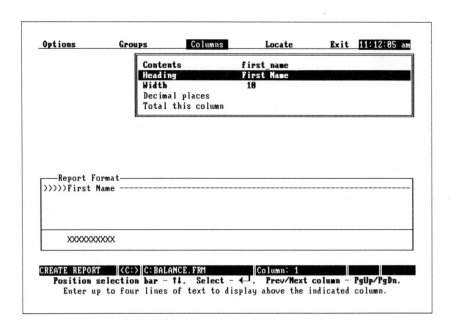

The final column in your report should hold the sum of the two balance fields. Enter **balance_1+balance_2** for the contents and **Total Balance** for the heading. dBASE will automatically sum the two balance fields to produce the total balance entry for each record listed in the report. In addition, at the bottom of the report, the program will total each of these three numeric columns. Your screen should now look like Figure 3.31.

Figure 3.31   Specifying Report Layout

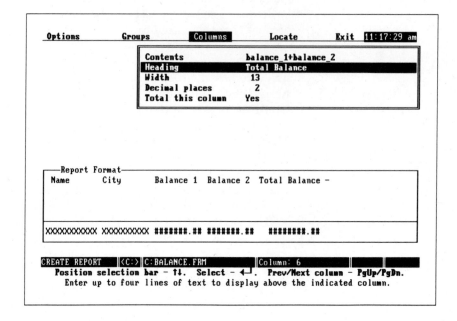

You've now finished specifying the report layout, so press the **Right Arrow** key twice to highlight the Exit option. Press **Enter** to save the report layout to the file BALANCE.FRM, and dBASE will return to the Assistant menu.

Step 3: Print the Report

Once you've set up the report layout file, printing the report is easy. Use the **Right Arrow** key to highlight The Assistant's Retrieve option. Now use the **Down Arrow** key to select the Report submenu option and press **Enter**. Select the disk drive on which your report layout file is stored, select BALANCE.FRM, and then press **Enter** to execute the command. dBASE will then ask you if you want to direct the output to the printer. If you have a printer, make sure it's turned on, line up the top of the page, and press **Y** for yes. If you don't have a printer, or if you just want to see the report on your screen, press **N** for no. Figures 3.32(a) and 3.32(b) show what you should see scroll by on your screen or on your printer paper.

Figure 3.32(a)   Kwik Key & Lock Customer Balances

```
Page No.        1
12/20/88
                    Kwik Key & Lock Customer Balances

First Name Last Name     City        Balance 1    Balance 2   Total Balance
Larry      Abel          Urbana         25.50        10.25        35.75
Barbara    Alexander     Champaign      52.00        25.75        77.75
David      Banks         Champaign      84.25        22.75       107.00
Molly      Becker        Savoy          12.25        58.00        70.25
Carrie     Calhoon       Tolono         23.50        14.50        38.00
George     Carver        Watseka        90.50        30.50       121.00
John       Crawford      Urbana          0.00        25.50        25.50
Irene      Daily         Urbana         45.00        54.25        99.25
Becky      Davis         Urbana         78.50        24.75       103.25
Jim        Diamond       Champaign      89.00        15.40       104.40
Candy      Eaton         Champaign      92.83        82.54       175.37
Barbara    Edwards       Paxton         92.95       123.00       215.95
Francis    Feldman       Urbana         29.23        98.23       127.46
Melissa    Franklin      Champaign      15.32        44.56        59.88
Gerald     Garret        Rantoul        25.84        72.33        98.17
Oscar      Griffith      Urbana         34.54        25.65        60.19
Robert     Hall          Pekin          22.33        52.41        74.74
Henry      Hudson        Champaign      43.88        23.43        67.31
Judith     Irving        Urbana         22.55        43.22        65.77
Delbert    Jackson       Monticello     38.22        41.55        79.77
Alfred     Jenkins       Champaign      22.11        51.37        73.48
Holly      Jordon        Danville       21.54        43.64        65.18
Joyce      Kelley        Tolono         25.00         0.00        25.00
Lesley     Knowles       Champaign      10.50        45.99        56.49
Terry      Lancaster     Champaign      52.75        23.53        76.28
Kim        Lee           Rantoul        10.25        25.50        35.75
Marcy      Lowrey        Urbana         25.75        52.00        77.75
Fred       Malony        Tolono         22.75        84.25       107.00
Ellen      McFall        Rantoul        58.00        12.25        70.25
Dan        Mitchell      Urbana         14.50        23.50        38.00
Scott      Nelson        Champaign      30.50        90.50       121.00
Sandy      Novak         Urbana         25.50         0.00        25.50
Roger      Olson         Champaign      54.25        45.00        99.25
Diane      Owens         Moticello      24.75        78.50       103.25
Charlie    Pearson       Tolono         15.40        89.00       104.40
Brian      Prorok        Champaign      82.54        92.83       175.37
Kerry      Quinlan       Rantoul       123.00        92.95       215.95
Mike       Reeves        Urbana         98.23        29.23       127.46
Ruby       Russel        Urbana         44.56        15.32        59.88
Julian     Savage        Savoy          72.33        25.84        98.17
Mike       Skubic        Champaign      25.65        34.54        60.19
Linda      Spencer       Urbana         52.41        22.33        74.74
Laurie     Townsend      Tolono         23.43        43.88        67.31
Anthony    Tudor         Champaign      43.22        22.55        65.77
Rhonda     Underwood     Urbana         41.55        38.22        79.77
Paul       Valentine     Monticello     51.37        22.11        73.48
Roxanne    Walden        Urbana         43.64        21.54        65.18
Sally      Weaver        Champaign       0.00        25.00        25.00
Allison    Willmann      Champaign      45.99        10.50        56.49
Susan      Young         Rantoul        23.53        52.75        76.28
```

Figure 3.32(b)   Kwik Key & Lock Customer Balances

```
Page No.      2
12/20/88
                    Kwik Key & Lock Customer Balances


First Name     Last Name     City     Balance 1     Balance 2     Total Balance


** Total ***
                                      2103.19        2103.19         4206.38
```

Lesson 13: Sorting the Data Base

One of the most common operations performed on data bases is sorting them into some particular order. Records are stored in a data base file in the order in which they're entered. This order is reflected by the record number assigned to each one. When we entered the records for the mailing list and customer balance data bases, they just happened to be in alphabetical order based on last names. If we add more records, however, all the records will no longer be in order. This is one reason why you might want to sort a data base. Another reason is that you might want to re-arrange records on the basis of some other fields. The sorting feature of dBASE III PLUS is both easy to use and powerful. It allows you to specify any number of keys on which to sort. As you may know, a key is a field that is used to order the records in a file. If you specify more than one key, the sorting is done successively on each key. For example, if you sort the mailing list data base first by city and then by last name, the records will be arranged alphabetically by city name and then alphabetically within each city by last name.

Step 1: Select the Sort Option

Use the **Right Arrow** key to highlight The Assistant's Organize option. Select Sort and press **Enter**. Your screen should look like Figure 3.33.

Figure 3.33   The Sort Option

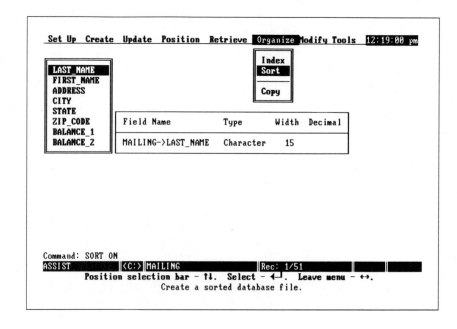

Step 2: Select the Fields on Which to Sort

The box at the left is a submenu of fields in the data base to be sorted. From it you're to pick the field or fields dBASE will use as keys on which to sort. Use the **Down Arrow** key to highlight CITY and press **Enter**. Now go back up to LAST_NAME and press **Enter** again. Your action line should say:

    Command: SORT ON CITY, LAST_NAME

This command is the dot-prompt command corresponding to the options you've selected; it tells dBASE to sort the mailing list on the basis of city first and then last name. Since you're finished specifying keys, press the **Right** or **Left Arrow** key to go on.

Step 3: Execute the Sort

You should now see a menu of disk drive letters on your screen. Choose the one on which your data base files are stored and press **Enter**. Now dBASE will ask you to supply a file name for the newly sorted data base. You must enter a new file name because dBASE creates a new file and sorts it according to your specifications. It's important to realize that dBASE doesn't alter your original file, MAILING.DBF. To name the new file, type **BY_CITY.DBF** and press **Enter**. The records from MAILING.DBF will be copied to BY_CITY.DBF, and alphabetized by city and then by last name within each city.

Step 4: Examine the Sorted File

To look at the new file, use the **Left Arrow** key to highlight the Assistant's Set Up option. Select BY_CITY.DBF as your current data base file. Again, press **N** for no when asked if the file is indexed. Now select the Browse option of the Update submenu. Your screen should look like Figure 3.34. Use **PgDn** and **PgUp** to traverse the records and see how they're grouped by city and then alphabetized within each city.

Figure 3.34   Scroll Through the Sorted File

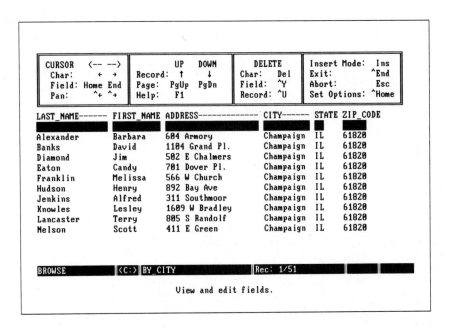

Lesson 14: Indexing the Data Base

If a data base has a great number of records with many fields, sorting it each time you want to rearrange it can take a long time. In addition, each time you sort a data base you end up with a completely new copy. If you have several versions of the same data base, each sorted in a different way, they can take up a lot of disk storage. Indexing can reduce these problems.

When you index a data base, you don't change the order of the records and the record numbers in the original file. Instead you create an index file that just lists the record numbers in the new order. With large data bases, the index file is usually much smaller than the data base file from which it's created. In addition, when you reindex a file, you have less data to move around so it doesn't take as long. As an analogy, think of a library as a data base. Each book on the shelf is like a record and the card catalog is the index. Each entry in the index, a single card from the catalog, lists the call number of a book. Now imagine that you had to arrange the books in alphabetical order based on the author's name. Which would you rather rearrange: the books themselves or the cards in the card catalog? What if you needed the books arranged in order of their titles too? If the books are indexed, you could just copy the cards, not the whole books, and have another card catalog arranged according to title. In fact, this is just what most libraries do.

Step 1: Select the File to Be Indexed

Let's return to working on your original mailing list data base. Use The Assistant's Set Up option to establish MAILING.DBF as the current data base file. We still haven't indexed it yet, so again press **N** when asked if the file is indexed.

Step 2: Select the Index Option

Use the **Right Arrow** key to move the highlight block to The Assistant's Organize option. This time, select Index and press **Enter**. Your screen should look like Figure 3.35.

Figure 3.35   The Index Option

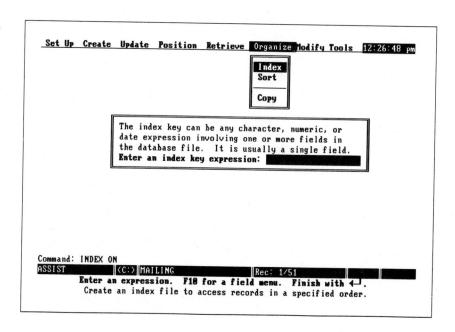

Step 3: Select the Index Key

Similar to a sort key, an index key is the field to be used as the basis for rearranging the record numbers. Although dBASE III PLUS lets you specify several fields for the index key, in practice it usually consists of only one field. Let's index the records of the mailing list data base on the basis of ZIP code. This approach would actually be useful if this were a real mailing list. It's also not exactly the same as sorting by city because larger cities may have many ZIP codes. At this point dBASE is asking you to supply the index key. Type **zip_code** and press **Enter**.

Step 4: Create the Index File

You should now see a submenu of disk drive letters on your screen. Select the one on which you have your data bases stored. This will be the disk on which dBASE will store your index file. Next you'll be asked to supply a file name. This is the name to be given to the index file. Type **ZIP** and press **Enter**. If you don't supply a file name extension, dBASE will automatically append .NDX to signify an index file. After the index file has been created, dBASE will tell you to press any key to continue work with The Assistant.

Step 5: Set Up the Indexed Data Base

The index file ZIP.NDX has been created, but the mailing list file MAILING.DBF has not yet been arranged internally by dBASE in the new order. To do this you must use The Assistant's Set Up option to establish MAILING.DBF again as your current data base file. This time, however, you get to answer **Y** to the question:

```
Is the file indexed? [Y/N]
```

You'll be presented with a list of index files from which to choose. Highlight ZIP.NDX and press **Enter**. This file is now considered by dBASE to be the "Master" index file. All records will be displayed according to the order of this index file unless you specify otherwise. Although only the master index file is actually active, you can also select up to six other index files if you have them. Then, if you make any changes to the data base, the master index file and any other inactive index files you've also selected will be automatically updated. When you're done selecting index files, press the **Left** or **Right Arrow** key to leave the menu.

Step 6: Examine the Indexed Base

To see the results of indexing the mailing list on the basis of ZIP code, select The Assistant's Update option and use Browse to view the records. Figure 3.36 shows how the records appear on your screen in order of increasing ZIP codes. Move the highlight block through the file and keep an eye on the status bar. Notice how the record numbers are not in order. Again, this is because the records themselves were not rearranged in MAILING.DBF; only the index file ZIP.NDX was reordered.

Step 7: Quit dBASE III PLUS

You are now finished with the lessons. Press **Escape** to return to The Assistant, press **Left Arrow** until the Set Up menu appears, highlight Quit dBASE III PLUS, and press **Enter** to return to DOS.

**Figure 3.36   Data Base
Indexed According to ZIP Code**

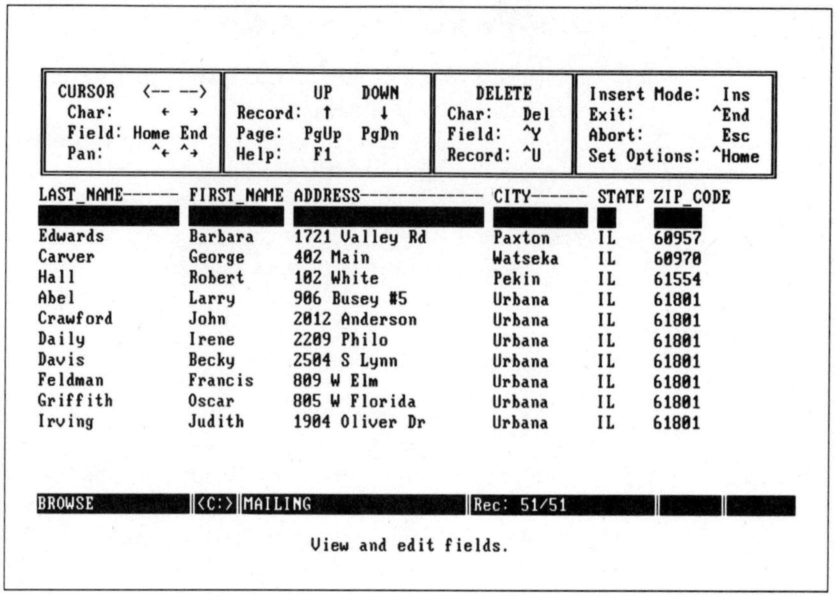

```
┌─────────────────────────────────────────────────────────────────────┐
│  ┌──────────────────┬──────────────────┬────────────────┬─────────────────────┐
│  │ CURSOR   <-- -->  │          UP  DOWN │  DELETE         │ Insert Mode:  Ins   │
│  │ Char:     ←   →   │ Record:   ↑    ↓  │  Char:    Del   │ Exit:        ^End   │
│  │ Field: Home End   │ Page:   PgUp PgDn │  Field:   ^Y    │ Abort:        Esc   │
│  │ Pan:      ^← ^→   │ Help:    F1       │  Record:  ^U    │ Set Options: ^Home  │
│  └──────────────────┴──────────────────┴────────────────┴─────────────────────┘

   LAST_NAME------  FIRST_NAME ADDRESS-------------  CITY------  STATE ZIP_CODE

   Edwards          Barbara    1721 Valley Rd        Paxton      IL    60957
   Carver           George     402 Main              Watseka     IL    60970
   Hall             Robert     102 White             Pekin       IL    61554
   Abel             Larry      906 Busey #5          Urbana      IL    61801
   Crawford         John       2012 Anderson         Urbana      IL    61801
   Daily            Irene      2209 Philo            Urbana      IL    61801
   Davis            Becky      2504 S Lynn           Urbana      IL    61801
   Feldman          Francis    809 W Elm             Urbana      IL    61801
   Griffith         Oscar      805 W Florida         Urbana      IL    61801
   Irving           Judith     1904 Oliver Dr        Urbana      IL    61801


   BROWSE           |<C:>|MAILING          |Rec: 51/51    |      |

                          View and edit fields.
```

Conclusion

In this chapter of the *Software Guide*, we've discussed some of the most important basic operations you need to know to use the dBASE III PLUS program effectively. However, this is an extremely large and complex software package. Entire books have been devoted to the subject, and the dBASE III PLUS documentation manuals are themselves several hundred pages long. There's much we didn't cover about dot-prompt commands not generated by The Assistant and the dBASE III PLUS programming language. These areas are, however, quite advanced topics. Perhaps you'll learn more about dBASE in other courses you take or at work. We encourage you to experiment and play with the program itself. After all, that process is how most people truly master the use of software packages.

Exercises

Multiple Choice

_____   1. A file is a collection of data that are organized into

(a) rows   (c) records

(b) columns   (d) bits

_____   2. dBASE III PLUS is a powerful data base management system that uses the

(a) relational model of data base   (c) network model of data base design
     design
                                           (d) distributed model of data base
(b) hierarchical model of data base   design
     design

_____   3. To run dBASE III PLUS, you would enter

(a) run   (c) go

(b) start   (d) dbase

4. dBASE III PLUS has an easy-to-use interactive menu system known as
   - (a) The Menu
   - (b) The Assistant
   - (c) The Shell
   - (d) The Manager

5. When you're using The Assistant, the very top line of the screen is called the
   - (a) message line
   - (b) action line
   - (c) menu bar
   - (d) status line

6. dBASE translates your menu selections into commands that are displayed on the
   - (a) message line
   - (b) action line
   - (c) menu bar
   - (d) status line

7. To invoke the dBASE III PLUS help facility, you press
   - (a) F1
   - (b) F10
   - (c) Esc
   - (d) Alt

8. To define the structure of a new data base, you use the Database file option of the
   - (a) Set Up submenu
   - (b) Create submenu
   - c) Update submenu
   - (d) Organize submenu

9. The following is *not* one of the allowed dBASE III PLUS data types:
   - (a) character
   - (b) numeric
   - (c) date
   - (d) integer

10. To select an existing data base, you use the Database file option of the
    - (a) Set Up submenu
    - (b) Create submenu
    - (c) Position submenu
    - (d) Retrieve submenu

11. Perhaps the easiest option for examining or modifying a small data base is
    - (a) Edit
    - (b) Display
    - (c) List
    - (d) Browse

12. To add new records to an existing data base, you would use the Append option of the
    - (a) Set Up submenu
    - (b) Create submenu
    - (c) Update submenu
    - (d) Modify submenu

13. If you know an existing record's number, you can most easily modify it with the
    - (a) Query option of the Set Up submenu
    - (b) Edit option of the Update submenu
    - (c) List option of the Retrieve submenu
    - (d) Format option of the Modify submenu

14. To remove deleted records permanently, you must highlight The Assistant's Update option and do a
    - (a) Replace
    - (b) Delete
    - (c) Recall
    - (d) Pack

15. To examine a particular record or a group of related records, use the
    - (a) Create option
    - (b) Update option
    - (c) Position option
    - (d) Retrieve option

16. If you want to search through an entire data base automatically and change one or more fields of selected records, highlight the Update submenu and use
    - (a) Replace
    - (b) Browse
    - (c) Display
    - (d) Edit

17. To change the record structure of an existing data base, use the Database file option of the
    - (a) Set Up submenu
    - (b) Create submenu
    - (c) Modify submenu
    - (d) Tools submenu

_____   18. To design a report layout, you must use the Report option of the
                                     (a) Create submenu   (c) Modify submenu
                                     (b) Retrieve submenu   (d) Tools submenu

_____   19. A field that is used to order the records in a file to be sorted is called a(n)
                                     (a) object   (c) index
                                     (b) key   (d) scope

_____   20. To sort or index a data base, highlight The Assistant's
                                     (a) Set Up option   (c) Organize option
                                     (b) Update option   (d) Tools option

Fill-in

1. A record is a collection of _____, each of which is a set of adjacent characters.

2. One or more files of efficiently stored, interrelated data items is commonly known as a _____.

3. A _____ data base organizes data elements into two-dimensional tables of rows and columns.

4. Most commonly used dBASE III PLUS operations can be performed by selecting _____ from menus rather than typing _____ that must be memorized or looked up.

5. Options are selected by using the _____ keys to move a highlight block on top of the desired choice and then pressing _____.

6. dBASE III PLUS has _____ types of data fields.

7. Data base records are input into a blank template, or _____ _____ _____.

8. The data base files created with dBASE III PLUS have a DOS file name extension of _____.

9. To look at the records of a data base a page at a time, you could use the _____ option of the Assistant's _____ submenu.

10. Several of dBASE's entry operations are terminated by pressing _____.

11. The Assistant's Position option lets you specify the number of the _____ record.

12. Every record in a data base is identified by its unique _____ _____.

13. A search condition is a set of one or more _____ that are applied to select certain records from a data base.

14. Letters of the alphabet are encoded by computers as numeric values that _____ in magnitude as you approach Z.

15. To update or delete records globally from a data base, you must make sure that the scope of the operation is set to _____.

16. To remove records from a data base permanently, you must first _____ them and then _____ the data base.

17. The Assistant's _____ option can be used to add new fields to an existing data base structure.

18. A formatted listing of the contents of a data base is usually called a _____ .

19. One of the most common operations performed on data bases is _____ them into some particular order.

20. When you index a data base, the order of the records and the record numbers in the original file are not _____ .

Short Problems

1. Look at the telephone directory for your city. Determine both the number of fields and the size of each field you'd need in order to use dBASE III PLUS for this data base. Be sure to design your fields so that any records from the directory will fit. This design will require some careful examination of several pages.

2. Consider the mailing list data base with which you've been working. Suppose the fifty records are all the file will ever contain, and that they'll never be modified. The data base structure could be changed so that some of the field widths are smaller. What new field lengths do you suggest using? How many bytes of storage space would you save by using these smaller field widths? (Remember that it takes one byte to hold one character.)

3. Use dBASE to search the MAILING data base file and display a list of records of customers who live in Tolono.

4. One of the Kwik Key & Lock customers is named Brian. Pretend you don't know his last name. How would you find his record? (Please don't suggest browsing through or listing the whole file!)

5. Let's say that you were looking over the customer receipts of the Kwik Key & Lock shop, and you noticed that one has the address as 305 Briar Lane. How would you go about finding the customer's name and the city, if this street address is all the information you have to go on?

6. When you sort a file using the Assistant menu, records are automatically arranged in ascending order. If you want to sort in descending order, you must use the SORT dot-prompt command. To sort the mailing list data base in descending order, you could enter this line from the dot prompt:

```
SORT ON LAST_NAME/D TO MAILING2.DBF
```

LAST_NAME is the key, /D indicates descending order, and MAILING2.DBF is the name the new sorted data base file that will be created. Try this out. Remember to press **Esc** to switch from the Assistant menu system to dot-prompt command mode. Enter **assist** from the dot-prompt to get back to the Assistant menu.

7. The Post Office has implemented a new nine-digit ZIP code, with the four new digits following a dash. For example, a ZIP code for Champaign, Illinois, might now be 61821–2398 (which will identify right down to the block). How would you modify the Kwik Key & Lock mailing list to accommodate this new ZIP code?

8. Determine the field names, types, and widths needed to design a data base to store information about your textbooks. Include not only title and author but also the price paid, the condition of the book, and what you could sell it for used. Be sure to use numeric fields for any dollar amounts.

9. Consider your collection of LP records, cassette tapes, and/or compact discs. Design a data base structure to catalog your holdings. In addition to the obvious fields like title, artist, and label, consider fields for the type of media (LP, tape, CD), condition, kind of music, cost, and year released.

10. A dBASE application that would be very useful to any homeowner would be a data base containing a list of personal property in the home. Such lists, which are usually arranged according to room, are especially helpful for insurance claims. Design a data base structure for a personal property inventory. Be sure to include fields for serial number, date purchased, and amount paid.

11. Go back to the Kwik Key & Lock BALANCE data base file. Let's say that you want to get the total of all customer balances for the first half of the year, but you don't want to generate a report. The Sum option of the Retrieve submenu can do this for you. Try it out. Then try the Average option.

12. Add to the Kwik Key & Lock BALANCE data base file a new field that will indicate if the customer has ever paid his or her bill with a check that bounced. Make up you own name for the field, but be sure to specify its type as logical. Remember, a logical field has only two possible values: T for true (or Y for yes) and F for false (or N for no). After you add the new field to the data base structure, use a global update operation to set every customer's field initially to false. Then go through the records and set the field to true for Weaver, Olson, Jordon, Franklin, and Calhoon.

13. Use the Display option of the Retrieve submenu to list all the records in the MAILING data base file, but only include the FIRST_NAME, LAST_NAME, and CITY fields in the presentation.

14. Modify the structure of the MAILING data base file to include fields for area code and phone number. You don't have to actually enter a phone number for each record, but use the Replace option of the Update submenu to give every customer an area code of 217.

15. In addition to appending records at the end of a data base, you can insert new records between existing records. The catch is that you have to use a dot-prompt command. Use the Locate option of the Position submenu to establish Holly Jordon's record as the current record. Press **Esc** to enter dot-prompt mode. Type **insert** and press **Enter**. You'll be put in EDIT mode to insert a record after Holly Jordon's. Make up some data and enter it. Now try another, but this time use **insert before**. Remember, to get back to The Assistant, type **assist** at the dot-prompt and press **Enter**.

16. Try tallying the total number of records in the MAILING data base with the Count option of the Retrieve submenu. Now build a search condition to count only those customers who live in Champaign.

17. It's the fifteenth of the month, but you're preparing a dBASE report that you want to be dated the last day of the month. Specifically, what do you do to get the correct date on your report? (Please don't say: "Wait until the end of the month to generate the report.") Hint: Where does the date that appears on the printed dBASE reports come from?

18. Secure a mailing label from any magazine that has been sent via mail, and devise a dBASE data base structure to produce such a label. Note that you'll have to guess at the maximum field widths.

19. Design and generate a report of the MAILING data base file.

20. You'd like to use dBASE III PLUS to organize the dates during the year when birthday, anniversary, and other cards should be sent to friends and relatives. Devise the data base structure for this application. You'll need fields for the occasion and the date of course. NOTE: Remember, the dates will need to be sorted.

Long Problems

1. dBASE III PLUS can store a large block of text (up to 4,000 characters) for each record in a memo field. This feature is ideal for creating a bibliographic data base. Choose some subject that interests you or that you have to do a term paper on. Design and create a data base of at least twenty of your reference sources. Be sure to include fields for author, title, publisher, copyright date, and notes. Use a memo data type for this final field and include in it descriptions and critical notes relating to the subject matter of the work.

2. Building on Short Problem 9, actually create and enter the records of your audio data base. Be sure to include a field for price paid. Sort you data base on the field of your choice and generate a report, complete with a computation of the total worth of your collection.

3. Even if you live in a dorm or rent an apartment, build on Short Problem 10 and actually create your own personal property inventory with dBASE III PLUS.

4. Traveling businesspeople must keep careful records of their expenses in order to be reimbursed or to claim them as deductions on their income tax forms. Airline tickets, automobile rental, mileage, meals, lodging, and supplies are a few of the possible expense categories. Design, create, and enter at least twenty records for a travel expenses data base.

5. If you're not now a "collector," there's a good chance you were as a child (coins, stamps, baseball cards, dolls, campaign buttons, slides, and so on). Create a data base for your particular hobby, and be sure to include fields for value and cost where applicable. Generate a sorted report and total all numeric fields.

6. Create an "electronic Rolodex." Build a data base to hold the information you keep in your personal address/phone book. Be sure to include fields for name, address, city, state, ZIP code, and phone number. If you want to, also include fields for work address and phone, birth dates, anniversaries, and any other information you ordinarily jot down. You might even include a memo field for more detailed personal notes.

7. Pretend you're a teaching assistant for one of the courses you're taking. Design and build a data base to keep track of grading. Be sure to include fields for each student's name, Social Security number, class, section, classroom, meeting day and time, homework assignments, tests, and final letter grade.

8. Create a data base for keeping track of the expenses associated with your (or your family's) car. Consider taxes, insurance, repairs, gas and oil, parking fees, tolls, and any other expenses (car washes, speeding tickets, and so on).

9. A dBASE application that may be useful to you long after you graduate is a data base that contains information on all of the courses you've taken throughout your college career. Build a data base that includes fields for course title, course number, semester or quarter and year taken, hours or credits earned, grade, instructor, and school (if you've attended more than one). Design it so that you can get dBASE to compute your grade point average.

10. Building on Short Problem 8, create a data base to store information about your textbooks, reference books, and personal books.

11. Use a current reference such as *The World Almanac* to create a data base containing the names of all the states' governors, U.S. senators, and members of the House of Representatives. Be sure to include a field to indicate their party and generate a report listing all the Republicans.

12. Don't put your copy of *The World Almanac* away yet! This time create a data base of information about the fifty states. Include state name, population, capital city, and area in square miles. Build a search condition to generate a report of all states with an area as big or bigger than Indiana. How about all states with a population at least as large as Alabama?

13. Use dBASE III PLUS to create your academic schedule for this semester. Include fields for the days, times, classes, buildings, rooms, and instructors. Generate a report of your class schedule.

14. Use dBASE III PLUS to create a weekly appointment calendar. Generate reports for the next few weeks.

15. No doubt midterms or finals are coming up soon. Create a data base that contains your test schedule, and generate a report.

16. Create a data base that contains a quick reference guide to DOS. Include a character field for each command you learned about in Chapter 1 and a memo field for a brief description of what that command does and how to invoke it. Sort the data base by command name and generate a report.

17. Look through computer books or magazines like *PC Magazine*, *Byte*, and *PC World* for information and reviews about data base management software. Create a data base containing at least twenty records of information about such packages. Be sure to include fields for name, manufacturer, price, copy-protected status, maximum number of fields per record, maximum number of bytes per field, and any other features you think are important.

18. Using the same types of sources you used in Problem 17, create a data base of information about at least ten spreadsheet programs.

19. Now create a data base of information about at least twenty word processing programs.

20. Impress your instructor! Design and create a data base of your own choosing –perhaps a collection of information for a hobby, personal interest, or career choice. Maybe your data base could involve some other courses you're taking, or something you find of interest in newspapers or magazines (stock markets, business trends, sports statistics, and so on). Be sure to include a brief write-up on what you're doing, and generate a report as well.

Software Installation

Most operating systems and application packages must be installed on your computer before you can use them. This typically involves running a special installation or setup program included with the software. Installation programs often create a new subdirectory on your hard disk, copy the files from the floppy disks included with the package to that subdirectory, and let you specify what kind of hardware you have. At most school microcomputer labs, this has already been done for you by the attendants. If you own a computer, however, you will probably have to install any new software you purchase yourself. The documentation that comes with the software should explain, step-by-step, how to run the installation program, and answer any questions that may be asked about your hardware and software. Let's briefly go over the steps necessary to install the software we discussed in this *Software Guide*: DOS and dBASE III PLUS.

MS- and PC-DOS Version 3.30

MS-DOS 3.30 and PC-DOS 3.30 are very similar. The MS-DOS package comes with two manuals entitled *MS-DOS User's Guide* and *MS-DOS User's Reference*. The first one contains the instructions for installing the system. The package can be purchased on either 3½-inch, 720K floppy disks, or 5¼-inch, 360K floppy disks. The 5¼-inch package comes with two disks, one labeled *Startup* and the other *Operating*.

Although the DOS 3.30 *Startup* diskette can be copied to another diskette to routinely boot up the computer from drive A, many people install the operating system on their hard disk C, if they have one. To install DOS 3.30 on a hard disk, follow these steps:

1. Insert the DOS 3.30 *Startup* disk into drive A.

2. Turn on the computer. If it is already on, press **Ctrl-Alt-Del** to reboot.

3. If the hard disk is not formatted (e.g., if you have a brand new computer), enter **format c: /s**. WARNING: Do not use this command if your hard disk is already formatted, or you will lose all files stored on it.

4. If the hard disk is already formatted with a previous version of DOS, enter **sys c:** instead of using the format command.

5. Enter **copy command.com c:** to copy the command processor to the hard disk.

6. If a subdirectory named DOS already exists on the hard disk, enter **del c:\dos*.*** to delete its contents. If such a subdirectory does not exist, enter **md c:\dos** to create it.

7. Enter **copy *.* c:\dos** to copy all the files from the *Startup* diskette to the DOS subdirectory on the hard disk.

8. Take the *Startup* diskette out of drive A, replace it with the *Operating* diskette, press **F3**, and press **Enter** to repeat the previous command and copy all of the files from the *Operating* diskette to the DOS subdirectory on the hard disk.

9. Remove the diskette from drive A, store all your original DOS diskettes in a safe place, and press **Ctrl-Alt-Del** to reboot your computer from the hard disk with DOS 3.30.

10. Enter **path c:\;c:\dos;** to set up the search paths for the root directory and the DOS subdirectory. You can add other search paths on the end of this command if you like. Ideally, this path command should be put in your AUTOEXEC.BAT file (see Chapter 2, Lesson 18).

IBM DOS Version 4.00

The DOS 4.00 package comes with two short manuals entitled *Getting Started with Disk Operating System Version 4.00* and *Using Disk Operating System Version 4.00*. The first one contains the instructions for installing the system. The package can be purchased on either 3½-inch, 720K floppy disks or 5¼-inch, 360K floppy disks. You should get the package with disks that match your floppy drive A. The 3½-inch package comes with two disks, one labeled *Install* and the other *Operating*. The 5¼-inch package comes with five disks labeled *Install*, *Select*, *Operating 1*, *Operating 2*, and *Operating 3*.

Although DOS 4.00 can be installed on floppy disks to boot up the computer from drive A, most people install the operating system on their hard disk C, if they have one. To install DOS 4.00 on a hard disk, follow these steps:

1. Insert the DOS 4.00 *Install* disk into drive A.

2. Turn on the computer. If it is already on, press **Ctrl-Alt-Del** to reboot.

3. After the copyright screen appears, press **Enter** and follow the instructions given by the installation program, which is called *Select*.

4. When you are finished with the installation program, remove the DOS floppy disk from drive A, store all your DOS disks in a safe place, and press **Ctrl-Alt-Del** to reboot your computer from the hard disk with DOS 4.00.

dBASE III PLUS Version 1.1

When you purchase dBASE III PLUS Version 1.1, you get two thick manuals in three-ring binders entitled *Learning and Using dBASE III PLUS* and *Programming with dBASE III PLUS*. You also get two small booklets named *Getting Started with dBASE III PLUS* and *Applications Generator dBASE III PLUS* and a small quick reference guide. The 5¼-inch package contains seven floppy disks:

■ **System Disk #1 and System Disk #2** These disks contain the actual dBASE III PLUS program.

- **Administrator #1 and Administrator #2** These disks are used to set up and run dBASE III PLUS on a local area network.

- **Applications Generator** This disk contains programs that let you create customized menu systems within dBASE III PLUS.

- **Sample Programs & Utilities** This disk contains data bases and programs used as examples in the manuals, and a utility program for converting dBASE II files to dBASE III PLUS format.

- **On-Disk Tutorial** This disk contains a program that teaches you about dBASE III PLUS.

To install dBASE III PLUS on a hard disk, follow these steps:

1. Turn on your computer and boot DOS.

2. Type **md \dbase** and press **Enter** to create a new subdirectory named DBASE on your hard disk.

3. Type **cd \dbase** and press **Enter** to switch to the subdirectory you've just created.

4. Insert *System Disk #1* into drive A.

5. Type **a:** and press **Enter**.

6. Type **install c:** and press **Enter**.

7. Follow the directions that appear on the screen.

8. Remove the dBASE disk from drive A, and put all of your original dBASE floppy disks away in a safe place.

9. Reboot your computer by pressing **Ctrl-Alt-Del**.

Glossary

adapter (also called an **expansion card**) a circuit board that connects a microcomputer to some external input or output device.

application package a program that enables a computer to accomplish useful tasks.

ASCII American Standard Code for Information Interchange; the code used by most microcomputers for storing text in binary form.

bit the basic unit of data processing; 0 or 1, on or off.

block any section of text, from a single character to a whole document, that can be marked and treated as a single entity.

boot up to load the operating system into a computer's primary memory and begin its execution.

browse to skim through the records of a data base.

bug an error or problem in a computer program.

bus a set of wires and connectors that link the CPU to memory and other computer components.

byte a contiguous group of eight bits; the amount of memory it takes to store a single character.

cell the unit formed by the intersection of one row and one column in a spreadsheet.

cell pointer in a spreadsheet program, the highlighted bar that marks your current location in a spreadsheet.

central processing unit (CPU) the part of a computer that performs calculations, logic, and control operations.

character any single letter, number, punctuation mark, or symbol. It is important to note that the computer interprets spaces as characters also.

chip see *integrated circuit chip*.

color graphics monitor a monitor that can display both text and graphics in more than one color.

computer an electronic device that performs calculations and processes data into information.

control panel lines at the top or bottom of the screen used to display information, messages, menu choices, and prompts.

color graphics monitor a monitor that can display both text and graphics in more than one color.

command processor the program in an operating system that translates and acts on the commands entered by the user.

computer an electronic device that performs calculations and processes data into information.

control panel lines at the top or bottom of the screen used to display information, messages, menu choices, and prompts.

CPU central processing unit; the part of a computer that performs control operations, calculations, and logic.

cursor a small, blinking underscore or box that marks the position where characters appear on the screen when typed.

cut and paste the process of marking a block of text and moving it from one location in a document file to another location.

daisy-wheel printer a printer with solid, raised characters embossed on the ends of little arms arranged like the spokes of a wheel; for producing slow, but letter-quality output.

data numbers, text, pictures, sounds that are to be processed into information.

data base an organized collection of one or more files of related data.

data base management package software that lets you create, add to, delete from, update, rearrange, select from, print out, and otherwise administer data files such as mailing lists and inventories.

debug to remove the bugs from an imperfect computer program.

default the predefined settings for certain features (margins, line spacing, column widths, etc.) that a software package uses automatically when alternate settings have not been explicitly established.

delete to remove, erase, or destroy one or more pieces of information.

desk accessory a utility program that provides commonly used desk functions such as a calculator, calendar, or address book.

desktop publishing the use of a computer and laser printer to produce near-typeset quality documents.

device controller a set of chips or a circuit board that operates a piece of computer equipment such as a disk drive, display, keyboard, mouse, or printer.

device driver a file in an operating system that contains the programming code needed to attach and use some special devices.

directory a list of the files stored on a disk; another term for subdirectory.

disk a medium, consisting of one or more flat surfaces on which bits are usually recorded magnetically, used by computers to store information.

disk buffer an area of memory that DOS uses to temporarily hold data being read from or written to a disk.

disk drive a computer system component that reads and writes programs and data on disks.

diskette a floppy disk.

display output screen on which the computer presents text and graphic images; monitor.

display adapter a circuit board or set of chips that controls a monitor.

document the paper output of a word processor.

documentation the user manual or technical information about a computer or software package.

document file a collection of text created by a word processing program in such a way that the text includes embedded formatting codes.

DOS disk operating system; an operating system that is stored on a disk.

DOS shell a program that enhances PC-DOS or MS-DOS.

dot-matrix printer a common type of printer that constructs character images by repeatedly striking pins against the ribbon and paper.

draft mode the fastest print mode, in which low-quality characters are formed by a single pass of the printhead.

edit to make changes to a file.

expansion board a circuit board that plugs into an expansion slot.

expansion slot an internal connector that extends a computer's bus and accepts an additional circuit board.

expert system a computer program that contains a collection of facts and a list of rules for making inferences about those facts.

export to produce a file with one software package that is ultimately to be used by some other software package.

field a group of related characters in a data base record.

file a collection of information stored on a disk and loaded into primary memory when needed by a program; in a data base, a group of related records.

file attribute a characteristic of a DOS file such as *read-only* or *archived*.

file locking a feature of DOS that allows only one person to use a file or part of a file at a time.

file sharing a feature of DOS that allows two or more people to use the same file at the same time.

filter a program that accepts data as input, processes them in some way, then outputs them in a different form.

floppy disk an inexpensive, flexible magnetic medium for storing computer programs and data.

floppy disk drive a disk drive that accepts floppy disks.

formula in a spreadsheet, an expression that performs some calculations and is stored in a cell.

function in a spreadsheet, a predefined formula that lets you perform a useful operation with a minimum of typing.

function keys on an IBM-compatible computer, the keys on the left side or top of the keyboard labeled F1 through F10 or F12. Such keys are usually used to perform common operations with different software packages.

global pertaining to or acting upon an entire document, spreadsheet, or data base file.

graphics any kind of graphs, plots, drawings, and other images not restricted to text characters.

hard disk a high-capacity, completely-enclosed, rigid magnetic medium for storing computer programs and data.

hard disk drive a disk drive that contains one or more hard disks.

hard hyphen a hyphen inserted into a document by the user that remains in the document even after it has been reformatted.

hard page break a division between two pages in a document, manually generated by the user, that remains in the document even after it has been reformatted.

hard return a new line or paragraph in a document, manually generated by the user, that remains in the document even after it has been reformatted.

hard spaces spaces in a document, manually inserted by the user, that remain even after the document has been reformatted.

hardware the physical components of a computer system.

hypertext software that lets you store and retrieve all kinds of information in a nonsequential manner.

IBM-compatible any computer that works like a comparable IBM model and can run the same software.

import to use a file in one software package that was originally produced in another software package.

incremental backup the process of backing up only those files that have been added or modified since the last backup.

index to arrange a list of record numbers in some particular order.

information a more organized and useful form of input data.

ink-jet printer a printer with a mechanism for squirting tiny droplets of ink to form text and graphics on paper.

input any data or information entered into a computer.

integrated circuit chip a thin slice of semiconductor material, such as pure silicon crystal, impregnated with carefully selected impurities; commonly used in computers and many other electronic devices.

integrated software a package that combines word processing, spreadsheet, data base management, communications, and graphics applications.

K the abbreviation for kilobyte; 1K = 1024 bytes.

key a field used to sort or index the records of a data base.

keyboard the device with which you type input into the computer.

label in an operating system, a word that marks the place in a batch file where a GOTO command is to branch to.

label in a spreadsheet, a text entry in a cell.

label-prefix character in a spreadsheet, a symbol that explicitly indicates that the succeeding text is to be treated as a label.

laser printer a high-quality printer that uses tightly-focused beams of light to transfer images to paper.

letter-quality like the output of a good electric typewriter.

load to copy a program or data file from disk into memory.

local area network (LAN) a system in which several microcomputers are connected together so that they can share hardware, software, and data.

M the abbreviation for megabyte; 1M = 1,048,576 bytes.

macro a sequence of keystrokes that can be entered, named, and replayed.

magnetic disk a semi-permanent storage medium that can be erased and written over and over again.

memory the part of the computer that stores programs and data temporarily.

menu a list of options available in a program.

microcomputer a small computer that uses a single microprocessor chip as its central processing unit.

microprocessor a central processing unit made up of a single integrated circuit chip.

modem *mo*dulator-*dem*odulator; a device that enables a computer to transmit and receive programs and data over ordinary phone lines.

monitor a computer display screen.

monochrome graphics monitor a single-color screen that can display both text and graphics.

monochrome text monitor a single-color screen that displays sharply-defined characters, but no graphics.

motherboard the main circuit board of a computer.

mouse an input device consisting of a small box with one or more buttons that is slid across the table top and allows the user to manipulate objects on the screen and select menu options.

NLQ near letter quality; a dot-matrix print mode that produces attractive output by having the printhead make two or more passes over each character.

numeric keypad on an IBM-compatible computer, the area on the right side of the keyboard arranged like the number keys on a calculator.

on-line connected to and controlled by the computer.

on-line reference a program such as a spelling checker, thesaurus, or user manual that you can use while running another program.

operating system the software that controls and supports a computer system's hardware.

output any information produced by the computer; the computer's responses to a user's input.

page break a location in a document file where a new page is to begin.

page layout software a program that lets you combine the output of a word processor and graphics program to produce documents on a laser printer.

partition a section of a hard disk that contains an operating system.

personal computer a microcomputer.

piping a feature of DOS, symbolized by the | (vertical bar), that allows the user to take the output of one command that would normally go to the display screen and feed it as input to another command.

pixel picture element; a tiny dot on a computer display.

primary memory where a computer stores the programs and data it is currently using.

printer a device for producing computer output on paper.

program a sequence of step-by-step instructions that run a computer.

programmer a person who creates computer programs.

programming language a set of symbols and rules to direct the operations of a computer.

project management package software to help you formally plan and control a complex undertaking.

prompt a symbol or statement that indicates the computer is waiting for a response from the user.

RAM Random Access Memory; the portion of a computer's primary memory used to store programs and data temporarily; also known as read/write memory.

range in a spreadsheet, a designation of contiguous cells.

read-only attribute a file attribute that, when turned on, prevents a file from being changed or deleted.

record a set of related fields in a data base.

redirection a feature of DOS, symbolized by >, <, >>, that allows you to send the output of a command to some other program or output device.

relational data base a data base that is organized in two-dimensional tables of rows (records) and columns (fields).

replaceable parameter a feature of DOS that allows the user to pass information to a batch file while it is running.

resolution the sharpness of a display screen.

right justification aligning text to the right margin.

ROM Read Only Memory; permanent primary storage that is encoded with programs and data at the factory, and can be read and used, but never erased, changed, or augmented, by the user.

scroll to shift what is on a computer display screen so that other areas are visible.

soft page break a division between two pages in a document that is automatically generated by a word processor; may be changed if the document is reformatted.

soft return a new line or paragraph in a document that is automatically generated by a word processor; may be changed if the document is reformatted.

soft spaces spaces between words in a document that are generated by a word processor to justify text in a document; may be changed if the document is reformatted.

software a program or set of programs that tells a computer system what to do.

software integration the sharing of data files between different software packages.

sort to arrange the records of a data base in some particular order.

spreadsheet a table of columns and rows of numbers, text labels, and formulas used in an electronic spreadsheet package for the manipulation of numerical, financial, and accounting data.

spreadsheet package software that lets you manipulate spreadsheets.

system board the main circuit board of a computer.

system software the software that handles the many details of managing a computer system.

system unit in IBM-compatible computers, the box that contains the central processing unit, memory, circuit boards, disk drives, and power switch for the system.

upwardly compatible an operating system or software package that adds new capabilities, yet retains all previous features.

utility a small, specific program that adds handy features to a particular operating system or application package.

windowing environment software that allows you to divide your screen into two or more boxes and run a separate program in each one.

word processing package a software package used to create, enter, edit, format, store, and print documents.

word wrap a word processing feature that automatically begins new lines when necessary without the user having to press the Enter key (carriage return).

Answers to Exercises

Chapter 1   The Microcomputer

Multiple Choice

1. c	6. c	11. a	16. c
2. a	7. c	12. b	17. d
3. d	8. b	13. a	18. c
4. b	9. a	14. b	19. b
5. a	10. d	15. d	20. c

Fill-In

1. IBM-compatible
2. processing
3. hardware
4. bus
5. RAM, ROM
6. hard disk drives
7. pixels
8. VGA
9. mouse
10. cursor
11. dot-matrix
12. software
13. languages
14. application
15. graphics
16. desktop publishing or page layout
17. integrated
18. windowing
19. project
20. expert

Chapter 2   The PC-DOS Operating System

Multiple Choice

1. c	6. a	11. d	16. a
2. b	7. c	12. b	17. b
3. a	8. c	13. c	18. d
4. d	9. b	14. d	19. c
5. d	10. a	15. b	20. a

Fill-In

1. files
2. PC-DOS, MS-DOS
3. memory
4. date, time
5. DIR
6. eight
7. classify
8. Escape or Esc
9. Ctrl-Break
10. prompt
11. CHKDSK
12. formatted
13. COPY
14. global
15. format
16. rename
17. ERASE or DEL
18. text
19. PRINT
20. MD or MKDIR, CD or CHDIR, RD or RMDIR

Chapter 3   dBASE III PLUS

Multiple Choice

1. c	6. b	11. d	16. a
2. a	7. a	12. c	17. c
3. d	8. b	13. b	18. a
4. b	9. d	14. d	19. b
5. c	10. a	15. d	20. c

Fill-In

1. fields
2. data base
3. relational
4. options, commands
5. arrow, Enter
6. five
7. data entry form
8. .DBF
9. Display, Retrieve
10. Ctrl-End
11. current
12. record number
13. comparisons
14. increase
15. ALL
16. delete, pack
17. Modify
18. report
19. sorting
20. changed